TOP **10**
MALLORCA

EYEWITNESS TRAVEL

Left **Palma Cathedral** Right **Valldemossa**

LONDON, NEW YORK,
MELBOURNE, MUNICH AND DELHI
www.dk.com

Produced by
Blue Island Publishing, London

Reproduced by Colourscan, Singapore
Printed and bound in China by
Leo Paper Products Ltd.

First published in Great Britain in 2003
by Dorling Kindersley Limited
80 Strand, London WC2R 0RL
A Penguin Company

**Copyright 2003, 2011 ©
Dorling Kindersley Limited, London**

**Reprinted with revisions 2005, 2007,
2009, 2011 (001)**

A CIP catalogue record is available from
the British Library.

ISBN 978 1 4053 5845 3

Within each Top 10 list in this book,
no hierarchy of quality or popularity is
implied. All 10 are, in the editor's
opinion, of roughly equal merit.

MIX
Paper from
responsible sources
FSC™ C018179

Contents

Mallorca's Top 10

The information in this DK Eyewitness Top 10 Travel Guide is checked regularly.
Every effort has been made to ensure that this book is as up-to-date as possible at the time of
going to press. Some details, however, such as telephone numbers, opening hours, prices,
gallery hanging arrangements and travel information are liable to change. The publishers
cannot accept responsibility for any consequences arising from the use of this book, nor for
any material on third party websites, and cannot guarantee that any website address in this
book will be a suitable source of travel information. We value the views and suggestions of
our readers very highly. Please write to: Publisher, DK Eyewitness Travel Guides,
Dorling Kindersley, 80 Strand, London, WC2R 0RL, Great Britain or email: travelguides@dk.com.

Jacket images: Front: **Getty Images:** DEA/G.SIOEN bl; **SuperStock:** Alvaro Leiva main. Back:
DK Images: Joe Cornish tc; Colin Sinclair tl, tr. Spine: **DK Images:** Colin Sinclair b.

Left **Angel, Sa Granja** Centre **Playa de Formentor** Right Read's restaurant, **Santa Maria del Camí**

Left **Santuari de Sant Salvador** Right **Inca**

Key to abbreviations
Adm *admission charge payable* **No dis acc** *no disabled access*

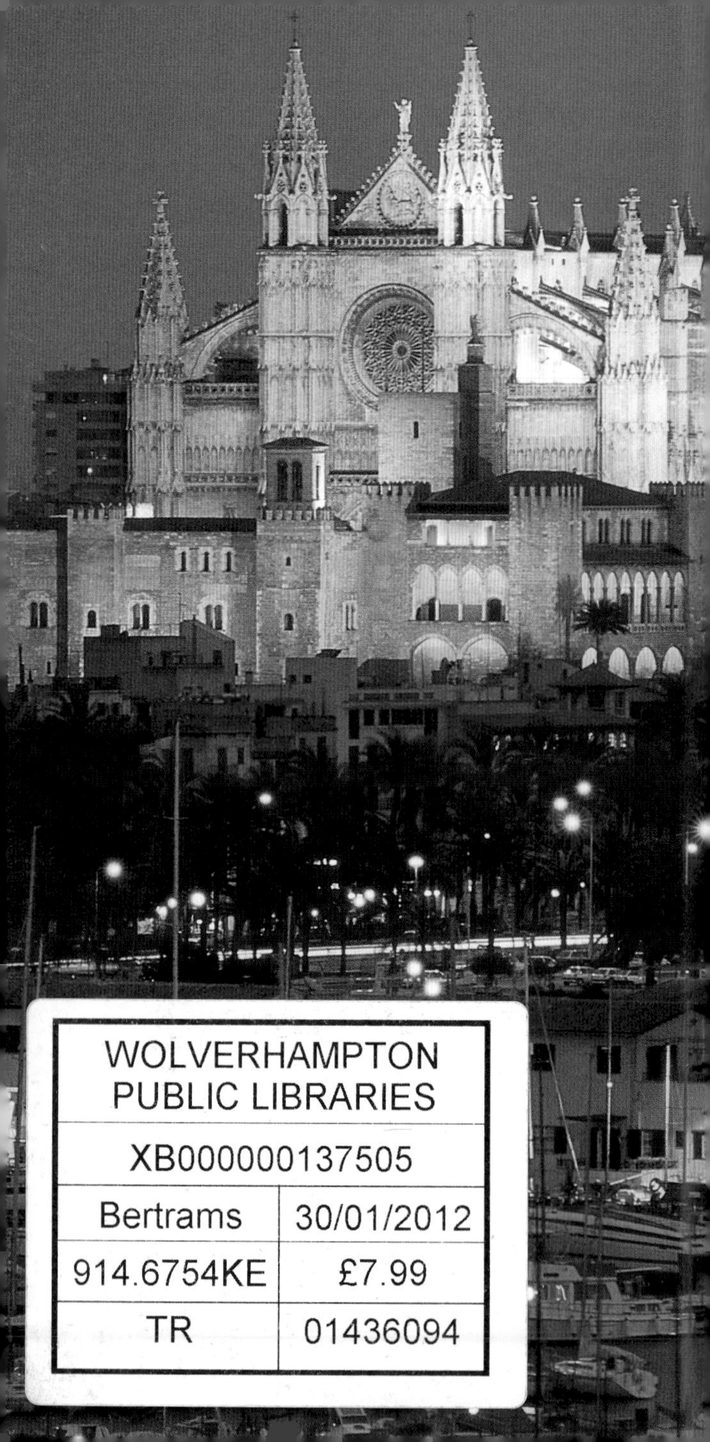

MALLORCA'S
TOP 10

Highlights of Mallorca

Known variously as the "Golden Isle", the "Wooded Isle" and the "Tranquil Isle", Mallorca is all of these, despite its decades-long dependence on mass tourism. The island is laden with history and sights, from its castles and enchanted gardens to caves and spectacular mountains. The eastern and southern coasts still sport some of the cleanest, most beautiful beaches in the Mediterranean, and the city of Palma is more attractive, culturally alive and fun than ever.

Mural, Valldemossa

1 La Seu: Mallorca Cathedral

Looming over Palma Bay, the Gothic cathedral's immensity is beautifully counterpoised by its soft golden colour and delicate filigree-like carvings. Among treasures within are the tombs of Mallorca's first kings *(see pp8–9)*.

2 Castell de Bellver

Standing sentinel on a hilltop, the castle of Bellver is immaculately preserved. Its walls have imprisoned queens and scholars, and they now contain an intriguing museum that evokes the island's past *(see pp12–13)*.

3 Fundació Pilar i Joan Miró

The genius and visionary power of the consummate Catalan artist are concentrated here. Not only can you experience the full range of Joan Miró's work, but you can also immerse yourself in the atmosphere of his studio *(see pp14–15)*.

4 La Granja

A mountain estate of gracious architecture and bucolic surrounds. Yet this peaceful haven is also home to a horrific collection of torture devices used by the dreaded Inquisition *(see pp16–17)*.

Valldemossa
5 Arguably Mallorca's most beautiful town, Valldemossa is where Polish pianist Frédéric Chopin and his lover, French writer George Sand, spent a miserable but creative winter in 1838–9 *(see pp18–21)*.

Jardins d'Alfàbia
6 Created by an Arab *wali* (viceroy) 1,000 years ago, these gardens include parterres, arbours and dells surrounding an all but derelict house. A great place for exploring and relaxing *(see pp24–5)*.

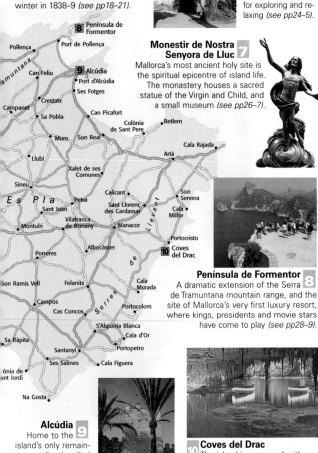

8 Península de Formentor
Port de Pollença
Pollença
Can Feliu
Crestatx
Campanet
Sa Pobla
Muro Son Real
Llubí
Sineu
Es Pla
Sant Joan
Petra
Montuïri
Vilafranca de Bonany
Porreres
Son Ramis Vell
Felanitx
Campos
Cas Concos
Sa Ràpita
Santanyí
Ses Salines
ònia de nt Jordi
Na Gosta

9 Alcúdia
Port d'Alcúdia
Ses Fotges
Can Picafort
Colònia de Sant Pere
Betlem
Artà Cala Rajada
Xalet de ses Comunes
Calicant
Sant Llorenç des Cardassar
Son Servera
Cala Millor
Manacor
Albocàsser
Cala Murada
Portocristo
10 Coves del Drac
Portocolom
S'Alqueria Blanca
Cala d'Or
Portopetro
Cala Figuera

Serra de Tramuntana

Serres de Llevant

Monestir de Nostra Senyora de Lluc **7**
Mallorca's most ancient holy site is the spiritual epicentre of island life. The monastery houses a sacred statue of the Virgin and Child, and a small museum *(see pp26–7)*.

Península de Formentor **8**
A dramatic extension of the Serra de Tramuntana mountain range, and the site of Mallorca's very first luxury resort, where kings, presidents and movie stars have come to play *(see pp28–9)*.

Alcúdia **9**
Home to the island's only remaining medieval walled city. It was built on the site of a Roman outpost, the theatre and ruins of which can still be seen *(see pp30–31)*.

Coves del Drac **10**
The island is peppered with fantastic caves, and these are the biggest and best. Spectacularly lit, the chambers echo with lilting classical music, played live from boats on one of the world's largest underground lakes *(see pp32–3)*.

Mallorca (or Majorca) gets its name from the ancient Roman name for the island, Balearis Major, meaning the "biggest Balearic"

La Seu: Mallorca Cathedral

The 14th-century cathedral is an imposing pile, with its Gothic buttresses, finials and bosses softly glowing in the sun. Legend has it that King Jaume I ordered it built in 1230, though in fact he merely modified an existing mosque. Work began in 1306 and has continued to this day. The western façade was rebuilt after an earthquake in 1851. Controversial touches were added in the 20th century by Antonio Gaudí.

The cathedral at night

⚓ The cathedral, as well as being the most important sight in Mallorca, is also a place of great religious importance, and tourist visits are not permitted during the celebration of mass *(see below)*.

🅾 Parlament, C/Conquistador, 11 (971 726026), is a Palma institution specializing in rice dishes, shellfish and stuffed asparagus.

Map L5 • Apr–May & Oct: 10am–5:15pm Mon–Fri, 10am–2:15pm Sat; Jun–Sep: 10am–6:15pm Mon–Fri, 10am–2:15pm Sat; Nov–Mar: 10am–3:15pm, 10am–2:15pm Sat. Mass: 9am Mon–Fri (with choir); 9am, 7pm Sat; 9am, noon, 7pm Sun • Adm €4

Top 10 Features

Portal del Mirador
The seaward, Gothic façade is the most spectacular side. Rows of ornate buttresses surround an elaborate door, which was formerly called the Door of the Apostles but is now known as the Mirador (vantage point).

Portal Major
Although it is Gothic in overall style, the main door *(above)* is mainly the product of Renaissance workmanship. A figure of Mary is surrounded by objects pertaining to her immaculate nature.

Exterior
Looking up from the old wall on the seafront, La Seu seems to have more in common with a craggy Mallorcan mountain than it does with any other European cathedral. It represents the might of the island's Christian conquerors.

La Seu, viewed from the west

Capelle del Santíssim
Designed by the renowned contemporary Mallorcan artist Miquel Barceló, the Chapel of the Most Holy boasts a large ceramic mural and fine stained-glass windows. The mural is loosely based on the miracle of the Feeding of the Five Thousand, with its remarkable, organic images of teeming fish and stacks of rustic loaves.

For the Palau de l'Almudaina, which stands opposite La Seu, see following pages

Bell Tower
5 This bell *(left)* is set within a three-storey-high tower surmounted with a "crown of lace" – a perforated parapet with small pinnacles. The structure is probably of Islamic origin.

Cathedral Plan

Entrance

Nave Columns
7 La Seu is one of Europe's tallest Gothic structures, and the sense of space in the interior is enhanced by graceful, elongated pillars that seem almost to melt away in the upper reaches of the nave *(above)*.

Rose Windows
8 A vibrant rose window *(below)* at the end of the nave is the main one of seven (a few are blocked up). Some say that the 20th-century "restoration" of the window's colours was too strong.

Gaudí Modifications
6 In 1904–14, the great Modernista architect set about improving La Seu's interior, removing mediocre altars and changing the lighting effects. The controversial baldachin *(below)* is actually only a mock-up – he never finished the final canopy.

Chapels
9 In all, there are 20 chapels, though some are now part of the chancel, with their altarpieces displayed in the museum. The tombs of Jaume II *(below)* and Jaume III are in the Trinity Chapel.

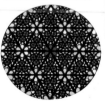

Museum
10 The collection includes some of La Seu's earliest altar panels, a polychrome wood sarcophagus, ornate reliquaries and furniture. Most mind-boggling are the pair of 18th-century Baroque-style candelabra, each as tall as a person.

Orientation
During the week, visitors must enter the cathedral through the museum on the north side (as it is a touristic, rather than a religious, visit). However, before taking in the interior of La Seu, walk around to the south side, facing the sea, in order to get a better feel for the awe-inspiring scale of the edifice.

For more on Mallorca's great churches See pp58–9

Left **Central Courtyard** Centre **Gothic Hall** Right **King's Rooms**

Palau de l'Almudaina

1 Function of the Palace

Stone lion outside the palace

Standing directly opposite La Seu, in an equally prominent position that actually obscures the cathedral's main façade from all but close-up view, this ancient palace adds a lighter, more graceful note to Palma's assemblage of civic buildings. Today, the palace is used for legislative and military headquarters, royal apartments and a museum.

2 Building Style

An amalgam of Gothic and Moorish styles, the palace has a unique charm. Square, medieval towers have been topped with dainty Moorish-inspired crenellations. Refined windows and open, airy arcades also tell of an abiding Islamic influence.

3 Central Courtyard

Known variously as the Patio de Armas, the Patio de Honor and the Patio del Castillo, this central courtyard also evokes a Moorish feel, with its elegantly looping arches and central stand of palm trees. A fountain incorporates an Islamic lion from the 10th century.

4 Hall of Councils

The largest room on the ground floor takes its name, Salón

de Consejos, from a meeting of ministers called here in 1983 by Juan Carlos I. There are 16th- and 17th-century Flemish tapestries, coats-of-arms and furniture.

5 Officers' Mess

The walls of this room are graced with beautiful 17th-century Flemish tapestries and genre paintings, some by a talented contemporary of Rubens.

6 Terrace and Banys Àrabs

Step onto the terrace for panoramic views. Then, back inside, peer into the remains of the Arab Baths. By means of mirrors, you can examine the three separate vaulted chambers below – one for hot, one for tepid and one for cold water.

7 Queen's Office

Taking the Royal Staircase to the upper floor, you encounter the Queen's Office, which

Terrace

The Palau is open Apr–Sep: 10am–5:45pm Mon–Fri, 10am–1:15pm Sat;
Oct–Mar: 10am–1:15pm & 4–5:15pm Mon–Fri, 10am–2pm Sat (adm €3.20)

Hall of Councils

contains fine antiques, tapestries and paintings.

King's Rooms

In these rooms you will find huge 17th-century Flemish tapestries, bronze statuary, Neoclassical paintings as well as some spectacular Empire furniture adorned with glittering ormolu fittings.

Gothic Hall

This remarkable room, noted for its huge pointed arches, is

Key to plans

Ground floor

First floor

used for official receptions. Don't miss the fine 16th-century Flemish tapestry on the back wall, depicting the Siege of Carthage.

Chapel of St Anne

The chapel's delicately coloured altarpiece, created in Barcelona in 1358, is a visual sonnet in sky blue and gold.

Typical Features of Traditional Houses

1. Kitchen fireplace
2. Clastra (main patio)
3. Cisterns
4. Tafona (oil press) and mill room
5. Defence tower
6. Capilla (family chapel)
7. Stone walls, floors and sometimes ceilings
8. Vaulted ceilings
9. Wood beams
10. Decorative motifs derived from Islamic, Gothic, Italian Renaissance, Baroque, Rococo, Neoclassical or Modernista styles

Stone arch entrance of a traditional house

Mallorca's Unique Architectural Heritage

Pointed stone arch, Gothic Hall, Palau de l'Almudaina

Stone is the keynote material in Mallorcan buildings of all kinds, whether in the form of natural boulders or carved segments. How those stones have been used has been a defining feature of the many cultures that have held sway on the island over the millennia. The Greeks, Phoenicians, Romans and Byzantines all left their traces and influences behind, however little may be in evidence. But what we mostly see today of pre-Christian traditions (especially in place names – most notably, any word with "al-") can be traced directly back to the Roman-influenced culture of the Islamic lords, who ruled the island during the 10th–13th centuries. In the ensuing centuries, something of that exotic style has been repeatedly renewed in Mallorcan building techniques and tastes, moulded into the Gothic, Renaissance, Baroque, Neoclassical, Modernista and even the most contemporary architectural styles.

For more on Mallorca's fascinating history see pp34–5

Castell de Bellver

This castle near Palma was a grand 14th-century royal fortress, royal summer residence and later royal prison. Surrounded for miles by fragrant pine woods, which are alive with whirring cicadas in the heat of summer, it also has stunning views over Palma Bay (Bellver means "lovely view" in Catalan). Looking up at this citadel, so perfectly preserved, it's hard to believe that it has been standing for 700 years. It is among the world's most striking castles.

View from battlements

View from tower

🕐 Avoid visiting the castle on a Sunday, when its excellent museum will be shut.

You can get to the Bellver hill by car or taxi, or take city bus 46 to Plaça Gomila and climb through the woods above Carrer de Bellver. Bus 50 stops at the castle.

🍴 La Posada de Bellver, C/Bellver, 7 (971 730739), is a friendly bar-restaurant offering a good-value lunch menu.

Map R1 • 3 km (2 miles) west of city centre • 971 730657 • Apr–Sep: 8:30am–8:30pm Mon–Sat (to 6:45pm Oct–Mar), 10am–6:30pm Sun (to 4:30pm Oct–Mar) • Adm €2.50 Mon–Sat, free Sun

Top 10 Highlights

1. Views
2. Circular Design
3. Defence Towers
4. Keep Tower
5. Central Courtyard
6. Prison
7. Museum Entrance and Chapel
8. Museum: Ancient Artifacts
9. Museum: Arab Artifacts
10. Museum: Spanish Artifacts

Views
1 Go to the top for a 360-degree panorama, including the foothills and sea to the west and the mountains to the north. The perfume of the pine forests creates a heady mix with the maritime breezes.

Circular Design
2 The elegant round shape is unique among Spanish castles and a premier example of 14th-century military architecture *(below)*. The circular structure also aided in the collection of rainwater into the central cistern.

Elegant stonework within the circular castle

Defence Towers
3 There are three horseshoe-shaped towers and four smaller protuberances used for guard posts. Their windows are tiny so that archers could not be targeted by attackers on the ground.

More marvellous castles and towers are on pp56–7

Keep Tower
The free-standing castle keep, called the *Torre de Homenaje (left)*, is almost twice as high as the castle itself, connected to its roof by a small bridge supported by a slim, pointed Gothic archway. It is open to visitors by arrangement (971 730657).

Entrance

Key to Castle Plan

	Ground floor
	First floor

Central Courtyard
The beautiful, two-tiered central courtyard *(left)* has 21 Catalan Romanesque arches on the lower tier, which contrast with the 42 octagonal columns supporting 21 Gothic arches on the upper tier. Classical statues, such as those of Venus and Nero, grace the lower walkway.

Prison
Right up until 1915, the lower reaches of the castle were used as a prison, dubbed La Olla ("the kettle"). Jaume III's widow and sons *(see p35)* were imprisoned here for most of their lives.

Museum Entrance and Chapel
From the central courtyard you enter Palma's Museu de Mallorca, in which sculptures *(right)* and other artifacts trace the city's history through Talaiotic, Roman, Arab and Spanish periods. The former Chapel of St Mark is now bare vaulted rooms.

Museum: Ancient Artifacts
The first three rooms contain impressive Roman statuary *(right)*, a perfectly preserved column of rare *cippolino* marble, carved seals, marble inscriptions, lamps and 1st-century pots.

Museum: Arab Artifacts
Surprisingly few remnants here beyond some pots, both painted and blue-glazed, a stone lion, terracotta lamps and *sgraffito* ware (pottery with etched designs).

Museum: Spanish Artifacts
A great range of styles and eras is presented, from medieval arms and a stone font with angels, dated 1591, to later works including 17th-century Mallorcan turquoise-glazed ceramics, Chinese porcelain, and items from the Belle Époque and Fascist eras.

TOP 10 Fundació Pilar i Joan Miró

The artist Joan Miró lived and worked on Cala Major from 1956 until his death in 1983. His wife converted the house and former studio into an art centre. This modern edifice, nicknamed the "Alabaster Fortress" by the Spanish press, is the work of Rafael Moneo, a

Carving, Miró's house

leading Spanish architect. It houses changing exhibitions from the museum's extensive collection, which includes many of Miró's paintings, drawings and sculptures as well as works by international artists.

Gardens in front of Miró's house

🚌 You can take the bus (EMT no. 3 and 6), taxi or drive to get to the Fundació, on a hill to the west of Palma.

An enlightening film on Miró is shown during the day (in Spanish); sometimes it is in English.

☕ The café is excellent, with made-to-order sandwiches, *pa amb oli* (see p78) and olives, fresh orange juice and more. It's also air-conditioned and features a wonderful mural by Miró (see entry 9).

• Map R2 • C/Joan de Saridakis, 29, Palma
• 971 701420 • May–Sep: 10am–7pm Tue–Sat, 10am–3pm Sun & hols; Sep–May: 10am–6pm Tue–Sat; 10am–3pm Sun & hols • Adm €6 (free Sat)

Top 10 Highlights

1. Building Design
2. Sculptures
3. Son Boter
4. Works on Paper
5. UNESCO's Mural del Sol
6. Works on Canvas
7. Temporary Exhibitions
8. Garden
9. Murals
10. Studio

Works in the Fundació's garden

1 Building Design
Composed of concrete made to look like travertine marble, the starkly modern building *(above)* is softened by reflecting pools, cool planes, ramps and staircases. Its high, narrow windows afford surprising views from the hilltop site. Most originally, huge marble panels are used as translucent walls, softly lighting the trapezoidal exhibition spaces.

2 Sculptures
Upon entering, you're greeted by three whimsical bronzes and a very much larger monumental piece, which are all vaguely anthropomorphic *(left)*. Downstairs, the giant *Woman and Bird* was executed by Miró with ceramist Llorenç Artigast.

3 Son Boter
This 18th-century estate was Miró's second studio. It is now used for courses and workshops given by international artists.

Works on Paper

Several works on paper are displayed *(above)*, most exhibiting the signature primary colours and splashes for which the artist is known.

Mural del Sol

Usually on display is a five-panel sketch on paper, the study for a mural in the UNESCO building in Paris, co-created with Llorenç Artigast in 1955–8. The work won the Guggenheim award.

Plan of the Fundació

Works on Canvas

Many of these works from the 1960s and 1970s are mixed media – oil, acrylic, chalk and pastel. Some may have been inspired by Japanese Zen action painting. Some are blue – for Miró the most universal and optimistic colour – while others are in black and white.

Temporary Exhibitions

The temporary exhibition spaces feature the works of international artists such as Louise Bourgeois, Adolf Gottlieb and Joan Fontcuberta.

Garden

In the garden, groups of rocks resembling water lilies "float" in a pool, while in other niches works by modern and avant-guarde artists can be found.

Murals

Above one of the garden pools, a black rectangle encloses a ceramic mural by Miró, with shapes gyrating in space. Taking up a whole wall in the café is a mural of the sun and other celestial bodies.

Studio

Miró's studio *(above)* looks like the artist just stepped outside for a break from work in progress. Objects that inspired Miró are all around: Hopi *kachina* dolls, Mexican terracottas, a bat skeleton and various everyday items.

Miró's Style

One of the best-known artists of the 20th century, Miró (1893–1983) was a Catalan through and through. Initially influenced by Fauvism, and later by Dadaism and Surrealism, he developed his own unique style, marked by lyricism and lively colouring. After arriving in Mallorca he became interested in graphics, ceramics and sculpture, scoring significant successes in every art form. The embodiment of a uniquely Catalan way of seeing the world, he became one the great exponents of Abstract Expressionism.

⊤10 La Granja

This possessió (country estate) is on a site known since Roman times for its natural spring. In 1239, the Count Nuño Sanz donated the estate to Cistercian monks; since 1447 it has been a private house. Visitors come today mainly to see rural Mallorcan traditions, such as demonstrations of lace-making, embroidery and spinning, and tastings of cheese, wine, sausages, doughnuts and fig cake.

Statue in courtyard

The house and grounds

🚗 The easiest way to get to La Granja is by car or tour bus.

Handicraft shows and horse and falconry displays take place from February to October on Wednesdays and Fridays from 3:30–5pm. Otherwise, visit in the morning to avoid the crowds.

🍴 The Granja Restaurant serves lunch all day, featuring *sopes mallorquines* (Mallorcan soup), and there's a snack bar/cafeteria. You can go for picnics within the grounds.

Map B3 • Ctra. Esporles-Banyalbufar, km 2, Esporles (between Valldemossa and Banyalbufar; follow signs off the main coast road, MA-1100) • 971 610032 • www.lagranja.net • 10am–7pm daily (to 6pm Nov–Mar) • Adm €12 adults; €6.50 children (4–12 years)

Top 10 Highlights

1. Gardens
2. Family Apartments
3. Dining Room
4. Loggia
5. Workrooms
6. Cellars
7. "Torture Chamber"
8. Chapel
9. Forecourt
10. Shows

1 Gardens

The cultivated areas are very rich, including a walled rock garden, moss-covered rock formations, botanical gardens, a pond with a water-jet fountain and a magnificent 1,000-year-old yew tree. You can still see some of the water canal that was used for irrigation.

2 Family Apartments

These rooms evoke the genteel country lifestyle of the house's former inhabitants. Of particular note are the curtains in the main room *(below)* made of *roba de llenguës*; the study with its curious old medical instruments; and the antique toys in the games room.

Fountain in the gardens

3 Dining Room

The main attraction here is the cleverly constructed dining room table that doubles as a billiard table. By turning the side crank, the height can be adjusted for both purposes. The crockery and glassware, from various eras, are original to the house, and the tile floor is also original.

Loggia

The loveliest architectural feature of the house evokes Florentine tenets of beauty and grace with considerable success. Providing a welcome breezeway on hot summer days and charming vistas at any time of the year, this porch-like gallery *(above)*, unusual in Mallorca, is a place to pause.

Entrance

Workrooms

The labyrinth of rooms downstairs comprises the earthy heart of the home. The estate was self-sufficient with its own oil-mill, tinsmith, winepress, distilleries (for liqueurs and cosmetics), woodworking shop, embroiderer and more.

Chapel

The altarpiece, with its lovely festooned arch, is Baroque; the altar itself a pretty Gothic creation; and the two kneeling, silver-winged plaster angels *(above)*, rather kitsch 19th-century efforts. Note the well-worn original tile floor.

Forecourt

The majestic space in front of the mansion contains four large plane trees that are about 150 years old. Here you can relax in their shade, watching craftsmen at work and sampling regional wines, liqueurs, juices, jams, *sobrassadas* (sausages), cheeses, figs, breads and *bunyolas* (potato flour buns).

Shows

Handicraft shows *(above)* and horse and falconry displays are staged on Wednesdays and Fridays.

Cellars

Cheeses were manufactured in the cellars, using the milk of cows, sheep and goats. Dough was kneaded using a stone mill, to make all types of pasta, for soups and other dishes. Dairy products, oil, wine and grain were all stored here.

"Torture Chamber"

A room displays the typical implements – including iron body cages and a rack – used against Jews, other non-Christians and suspected heretics or witches during the Spanish Inquisition of the 15th–17th centuries. Vicious-looking chastity belts are also on display.

Traditional Music and Dancing

Fashioned from wood and animal skins, Mallorcan instruments include the *xeremia* (bagpipe), *fabiol* (flute), *tamborino* and *guitarro*. Typical famous dances are the Bolero (18th century), La Jota (from eastern Mallorca), the Fandango (a line dance), Copeo and Mateixa (both also from the east). Many dances are improvised, accompanied only by percussion instruments; a more organized ensemble will perform on formal occasions.

⁵⁰⁰ Valldemossa

This small, picturesque town in the mountains is arguably where Mallorcan tourism began one cold winter in 1838, when the composer Frédéric Chopin and his lover, the female writer George Sand, rented some rooms at the former monastery here. Shunned by locals, the couple had a miserable time, as portrayed in Sand's book, A Winter in Majorca. *However, Mallorcans today are proud of their Chopin-Sand connection, and the book is sold in every tourist shop.*

Palace of King Sanç

🔲 The best views of the town, with its beautiful green-tiled bell tower, are those as you approach from the north.

If you arrive by car, park in one of the municipal car parks with automatic meters, then explore the town on foot.

🔲 One of the most developed tourist towns in Mallorca, Valldemossa has many good dining options. Es Port (Ctra. Port de Valldemossa, 971 616194) offers a superb Mediterranean-style menu and great views.

Map C3 • Monastery and Museum Mar–Oct: 9:30am–6pm Mon–Sat, 10am–1:30pm Sun; Nov–Feb: 9:30am–4:30pm Mon–Sat
• 971 612148 (museum)
• Adm €6.95 for both

⁴ Monastery: Pharmacy

Laden with tinctures and elixirs, a deconsecrated chapel recreates the estate's original pharmacy. George Sand *(portrait above)* bought marshmallow here in an attempt to cure Chopin's tuberculosis.

Top 10 Sights

1. Former Monastery Complex
2. Monastery: Church
3. Monastery: Cloisters
4. Monastery: Pharmacy
5. Monastery: Prior's Cell
6. Monastery: Cells 2 and 4
7. Monastery: Palace
8. Old Town
9. Church of Sant Bartomeu
10. Birthplace of Santa Catalina Thomàs

¹ Former Monastery Complex

The town's top attraction is the former monastery where Chopin and Sand stayed, which also incorporates a palace and an excellent municipal museum *(see pp20–21)*. Given to the Carthusian Order in 1399, the estate was a monastery until 1835, when all religious orders were ousted from the island. It was bought by a French banker who rented the rooms to Chopin.

² Monastery: Church

The Neoclassical church has a cupola decorated with frescoes by Fray Bayeu, the brother-in-law of Francisco de Goya. It is distinguished by barrel vaulting and gilt-edged stucco work.

The town viewed from the north

³ Monastery: Cloisters

From the church, you can enter the atmospheric cloisters *(above)*, known as the Myrtle Court. Around them are six chapels and ten spacious monks' cells.

The former monastery, also referred to as the Charterhouse, is Mallorca's second most-visited building after Mallorca cathedral

Monastery: Cells 2 and 4
Said to be the rooms that Chopin and Sand rented *(left)*, they are full of memorabilia, including Chopin's piano, Sand's manuscripts, busts *(below)* and portraits.

Monastery: Prior's Cell
The head monk had a private oratory, magnificent library, elegant audience chamber, bedroom, dining room, Ave María (praying alcove) and, of course, a sumptuous garden.

Monastery: Palace
The core of the monastery was originally the site of the palace built by Jaume II for his son Sanç. The rooms are regally decorated – an especially beautiful piece is the 12th-century woodcarving of the Madonna and Child.

Old Town
The old town *(below)* spills down a hillside, surrounded by farming terraces and *marjades* (stone walls) created 1,000 years ago by the Moors. The name "Valldemossa" derives from that of the original Moorish landowner, Muza.

Church of Sant Bartomeu
Near the bottom of the old town, a rustic, Baroque-style church is dedicated to one of the patron saints of the town. It was built in 1245, shortly after Jaume I conquered Mallorca, and extended in the early 18th century. The bell tower and façade date from 1863.

Birthplace of Santa Catalina Thomás
Mallorca's only saint, Catalina Thomàs (known affectionately as the "Beatata" for both her saintliness and diminutive stature), was born in 1533 at a house on C/Rectoría, 5. The house was converted into an oratory in 1792 and features saintly scenes *(above left)* and a statue of the "Beatata" holding a bird.

For highlights of the Museu Municipal de Valldemossa, which is set within the former monastery, see following pages

Left **Hapsburg-Lorena family tree** Right **Central room**

Museu Municipal de Valldemossa

1 Guasp Printworks

On the ground floor of the museum you'll find a 17th-century hand press and one of Europe's finest collections of 1,584 intricate boxwood engravings. On the walls are prints executed on the press, which is still in working order.

Printing press

2 Archduke Luis Salvador of Hapsburg-Lorena and Bourbon

Also on the ground floor is a room dedicated to an indefatigable chronicler of Mediterranean life, whose passion was Mallorcan culture. His nine volumes on the Balearics are the most exhaustive study ever made of the archipelago.

3 Mallorcan Painters of the Tramuntana

Mallorca's mountainous Tramuntana region has long attracted landscape painters.

Among the outstanding Mallorcan artists shown here are Joan Fuster, Bartomeu Ferrà and Antoni Ribas.

4 Catalan and Spanish Painters of the Tramuntana

Works by Sebastià Junyer, and the more Impressionistic Eliseo Meifrén are displayed.

5 International Painters of the Tramuntana

These include contemporary Italian master Aligi Sassu, whose works owe much to Futurism, Surrealism and Expressionism.

6 Contemporary Art: Juli Ramis

The contemporary collection was conceived as a spotlight on Juli Ramis (1909–90), one of the most important Mallorcan painters of the 20th century. Works include his signature *Dama Blava* and those of his Paris contemporaries, showing a cross-fertilization of influences.

7 Miró

Of note is *El Vol de l'Alosa* (Flight of the Swallows) – Miró's whimsical illustrations for the works of Mallorcan poets.

Painting by the Mallorcan artist Joan Fuster

The Museu is located on two floors within Valldemossa's former monastery complex – see previous pages

8 Picasso

Sadly, Picasso's masterful reworking of El Greco's great painting *The Burial of Count Orgaz* has been removed from the collection. However, there are still several paintings of bulls and bullfighters as well as some fine book illustrations.

9 Tàpies

Also in the last room are a few works by another great Catalan painter, Antoni Tàpies. Master of an elegant Abstract Expressionism all his own, his work has little in common with the more Surrealistic images of his compatriots Miró and Dalí, being more understated, poetic and monumental.

10 Other 20th-Century Artists

Finally, there are some small but significant engravings and lithographs by modern international artists, including German Surrealist Max Ernst, Italian Futurist Robert Matta, French Dadaist André Masson and the English masters Henry Moore and Francis Bacon.

Cultural and Ecological Attractions

1 **Public nature parks**
S'Albufera, Mondragó, Sa Dragonera, Cabrera, S'Albufereta Nature Reserve, Serra de Llevant

2 **Private nature parks**
La Reserva Puig de Galatzo, Natura Parc, Botanicactus, Jumaica Tropical Park

3 **Agroturism**

4 **Rural hotels**

5 **Centres for traditional culture**
Sa Granja, Els Calderers, Jardins d'Alfàbia, Raixa, Gordiola Glassworks

6 **Archaeological and historical museums**

7 **Accommodation in monasteries**

8 **Mountain shelters**

9 **Animal rescue and endangered species programmes**
Marineland

10 **Proposed parks**
Serra de Tramuntana

From Mass Tourism to Culture and Ecology

Preserved lamp and mural, Valldemossa

Most fittingly, since Mallorcan tourism got its shaky start here in the early 19th century, it is also in Valldemossa that it is being taken to a new level in the 21st century. Movie stars Michael Douglas and Catherine Zeta Jones own a big estate and founded the Costa Nord de Valldemossa (it is now run by the Balearic government). This multifaceted organization promotes both cultural and ecological tourism on an island that, to many, went too far in catering to cheap sun-sand-surf packages in the past. All over the island is an ever-increasing number of nature parks, museums and wonderful inland hotels at all price levels.

Agroturism: Sa Pedrissa *(see p145)*, Deià

Following pages **Palau de l'Almudaina, Palma**

TOP 10 Jardins d'Alfàbia

A legacy of the Moorish talent for landscaping and irrigation, the Jardins d'Alfàbia were probably designed by Benhabet, a 13th-century Muslim governor of Inca. The pleasures of the gardens are made possible by a spring that always flows, even in the driest of summers in this very arid land. As well as providing a fabulous oasis for visitors, Alfàbia is also a working farm.

Gardens and mountains

Top of terraced cascade

Top 10 Highlights

1. Entrance and Gatehouse Façade
2. Terraced Cascade
3. Queen's Bath
4. Pergola and Walkway
5. English-Style Gardens
6. Trees
7. Groves
8. Hacienda
9. Flemish Armchair
10. Courtyard

🔾 The arcing waters of the pergola walkway are operated from a button at the start of the display. However, be aware that the stones under the arbour can become very slippery.

Books and postcards can be purchased at the entrance ticket room or snack bar.

🔾 The garden snack bar offers delicious fresh juices, nuts and dried fruit, and other simple, refreshing tidbits, much of it from the farm itself.

Map C3 • Ctra. de Sóller, km 17, Bunyola (just off main highway MA-11, before toll booth for the Sóller tunnel)
• 971 613123 • 9am–5:30pm Mon–Fri; Apr– Oct to 6:30pm and also 9am–1pm Sat
• Adm €4.50

1 Entrance and Gatehouse Façade

A broad ramp leads past a moss-covered fountain to a Baroque façade, which is set off with palm trees, scrolling arabesque curves and a pair of windows *(above)* called *ojo de buey* (ox-eye).

2 Terraced Cascade

To the left of the gatehouse façade is a stepped, terraced cascade *(right)*. Watercourses, called *alfagras* (little irrigation channels), serve both a practical and a decorative purpose here and in other Moorish-style gardens.

Paved walkway with water jets

3 Queen's Bath

An open-ended cistern frames a mirror-like pool, called the "queen's bath", which is the source of all the water in the gardens. Beyond it is an indescribably lush garden scene.

For more beautiful parks and gardens in Mallorca See pp64–5

4 Pergola and Walkway

From an eight-sided pergola, a paved walkway is lined with ancient amphorae shooting out jets of water. Between column pairs four and five, don't miss greeting the black Mallorcan pig.

5 English-Style Gardens

These were created in the 19th century and feature bougainvillea, vines, box hedges, scarlet dahlias and a lily pond. Farm products are sold at a snack bar.

6 Trees

An extraordinary range of trees flourishes in the gardens, including white fir, maple, cedar of Lebanon, Monterey cypress, poplar, date palm, holm oak, carob, lemon, magnolia, walnut, eucalyptus and acacia.

Plan of the Gardens and Buildings

7 Groves

These magical areas are given over to dense plantings in which you can lose yourself, with the refreshing sound of running water always playing in your ears. Hidden pools and ancient walls are among the discoveries to be made.

8 Hacienda

After exploring the gardens, make your way up the hill to the wisteria-covered, L-shaped hacienda with Doric columns. Inside, traditional *llengues* (flame) fabrics, old prints, instruments *(above)* and a guitar-shaped grandfather clock are among the exhibits.

9 Flemish Armchair

Also in the hacienda is one of the oldest and oddest pieces of furniture on the island *(left)*. This 15th-century oak chair has been known, among other things, as the Moorish King's Chair, but the imagery on it has now been identified as the story of Tristan and Isolde. See if you can spot the king's head.

10 Courtyard

The courtyard *(right)* features a huge, 100-year-old plane tree and a moss-covered fountain. From here, you can visit some of the other rooms, then exit through a pair of vast, bronze-covered hobnailed doors, which were originally those of the Palace of the Inquisition in Palma.

🔟 Monestir de Nostra Senyora de Lluc

The monastery at Lluc is the spiritual centre of Mallorca and has been a place of pilgrimage for over 800 years. The main point of interest is the little statue of the Virgin (La Moreneta), which, so the story goes, was found by an Arab shepherd boy who had converted to Christianity. The image was initially moved to the church but it kept returning to the same spot, so a chapel was built to house it. Each year, thousands of pilgrims come to pay homage.

La Moreneta ("the Little Dark One")

Top 10 Highlights

1. The Complex
2. Basilica Entrance
3. Basilica Interior
4. La Moreneta
5. Es Blavets
6. Museu de Lluc
7. Museum: Religious Artifacts
8. Museum: Majolica
9. Els Porxets
10. El Camí dels Misteris del Rosari

Basilica façade

🔂 After you've visited the monastery, explore some of the natural areas and caves nearby, some of which are prehistoric burial sites.

🔂 Head for Sa Fonda, in the erstwhile monks' grand dining room, which offers Mallorcan fare (closed in July). Otherwise, try the Café Sa Plaça for snacks, or the Restaurant Ca S'Amitger, Plaça Peregrins, 6, where you'll find *tortilla espanyola*, fish, roast lamb, mountain goat and rice *brut*, a Mallorcan country dish.

• Map D2 • Museu de Lluc 10am–1.30pm, 2:30–5:15pm • 971 871525 • Adm €3

Courtyard within the complex

The Complex
The complex is rather plain but set amid fragrant forests of pine and holm oak, and laid out around courtyards. There's a good hostel, choir school, several eateries, camp sites, picnic facilities and a huge covered area for outdoor celebrations and services.

Basilica Entrance
Facing an inner courtyard, the church's façade is an appealing Baroque confection that relieves the plainness of the surrounding structures. The pompous bronze statue that dominates is that of a bishop who had a hand in sprucing the place up in the early 1900s.

Basilica Interior
The church *(left)* was deemed a Minor Basilica by the Pope – its embellishments are probably the reason. Every spare inch seems to have been laden with beaten gold. The columns are dark red jasper, crystal chandeliers light the way, and the altarpiece is alive with golden curves and gesticulating figures.

La Moreneta

In a special chapel stands the object of pilgrimage, La Moreneta ("the Little Dark One") – or, to be more precise, a 15th-century, possibly Flemish, version of her. Unfortunately, the 1960s light fixtures in the chapel detract from the atmosphere.

Els Blauets

The boys' choir, Els Blauets (The Blues), was established in 1531, named after their blue cassocks. Pilgrims and tourists queue up at 11am to hear the daily concerts.

Museu de Lluc

A broad collection of Mallorcana includes prehistoric and ancient artifacts, coins, religious treasures, vestments, sculptures, ceramics and paintings, as well as model Mallorcan rooms from the 17th century.

Museum: Majolica

In the 15th century, Italy imported large amounts of tin-glazed pottery from Spain by way of the trade route through Mallorca, hence the term "majolica" from the medieval name of the island. Until the early 20th century, this type of pottery was also produced in Mallorca. Various examples are displayed.

Els Porxets

The gallery of the old pilgrim's hospice is a picturesque arcaded corridor, with stables on the ground floor and bedrooms off the passageway on the upper level. Declared a Historical Artistic Monument, it has been carefully restored.

Museum: Religious Artifacts

Pieces on display include a fabulous gilded Byzantine *trikerion* (three-part sacred utensil) from 1390, a 15th-century wooden tabernacle, a graceful 15th-century Flemish Virgin and Child *(left)*, a gold filigree reliquary for a Piece of the True Cross and several devotional paintings.

El Camí dels Misteris del Rosari

"The Way of the Mysteries of the Rosary" is a pilgrim's route leading up the rocky hillside behind the complex, where a crucifix awaits. The broad path *(right)* is punctuated by bronze sculptures framed in stone.

For other great churches and monasteries see pp58–61

Península de Formentor

The final jutting spur of the Serra de Tramuntana has stunning views, sandy beaches and the island's original luxury resort. With weird rock formations and jagged edges pointing up at 45 degrees, its mountains rise to over 400 m (1,300 ft). The drive from Port de Pollença has dramatic scenery and is famously scary for its steep bends.

Watchtower ruins

🕐 To avoid the heaviest traffic, visit early or late in the day. If you take the road up to the Watchtower, park at the turnout just after the first bunkers, slightly down from the top. That way you'll avoid the parking snarls at the top.

🍽 The Lighthouse snack bar has pizzas, sandwiches, olives and drinks of all kinds. Sit on the broad terrace for incredible views.

For something more refined, as well as far more expensive, head for the Hotel Formentor's beach restaurant on your way back.

• Map F1

Top 10 Highlights

1. Peninsula Road
2. Main Miradors
3. Watchtower
4. Beach
5. Hotel Barcélo Formentor
6. Casas Velles
7. Mountain Tunnel
8. Cap de Formentor
9. Lighthouse
10. Flora and Fauna

1 Peninsula Road
The famous road *(above)* is narrow but well maintained, forking off to the Hotel Formentor in one direction and across to the cape in the other. Side-roads along the way – sometimes much rougher – wind up to the Watchtower and give access to the beach, as well as makeshift car parks for Cala Figuera.

2 Main Miradors
Of the main *miradors* (viewpoints), Mirador de Mal Pas *(above)* is closest to the road. From here you can walk along a wall with dizzying panoramas of the rocks and sea below. You can also see the islet of Es Colomer.

View from Mirador des Colomers

3 Watchtower
The Talaia d'Albercutx *(below)* has an amazing view over the Peninsula and bays of Pollença and Alcúdia. But the road to it is very bad, without guardrails, so hire a four-wheel drive if you can. For a further adrenalin rush, you have to hike up the last bit and climb the tower itself.

Beach

In a long, sheltered cove with fine sand and clear turquoise water *(above)*, Platja de Formentor is served both by road and a regular ferry from the Port de Pollença. Eating spots and *tiki* shades abound. Expect crowds of families at weekends.

Hotel Barceló Formentor

The posh resort *(right)* opened in 1929 and has been pampering the rich and famous ever since *(see p141)*. Part of the Platja de Formentor is reserved for hotel guests only.

Casas Velles

An old Mallorcan house is preserved in the grounds of the Hotel Formentor. There's a characteristic courtyard with an old stone well, a one-room house and a chapel with a melodramatic, life-size crucifix.

Mountain Tunnel

The road continues through pine woods and past more *miradors* on its way to En Fumat mountain. It then tunnels through the raw rock of the mountain. For those who need more thrills, there's a steep staircase up the cliff above the tunnel's western mouth.

Cap de Formentor

The terrain becomes rockier towards the end of the peninsula, and soon you have a plunging view down to Cala Figuera, Mallorca's most inaccessible beach, where a few boats have anchored. It's a harrowing drive out to the end, but you're rewarded with breathtaking views *(right)*.

Lighthouse

Around the last curve, you come upon the silver-domed lighthouse *(left)*, set on a dramatic promontory with views over the sea. On a good day, you can see all the way to Menorca.

Flora and Fauna

The peninsula is all wild: pine trees mostly, with scrub and clump grasses, oregano, cactus and wild palmetto everywhere. On a hot summer's day, with cicadas buzzing, you'll see wild goats, lizards and birds.

For more areas of natural beauty **see pp36–7**

⑩ Alcúdia

At the base of a peninsula, this delightful walled town was originally a Phoenician settlement and the capital of the island under the Romans. It was later destroyed by the Vandals, then rebuilt by the Moors, and prospered as a trading centre well into the 19th century. Extensively restored, the town contains many historical sites of interest.

Port d'Alcúdia

Grand Café, port area

🚗 If you are arriving by car, you should find ample parking just outside the old walls.

🍴 Es Canyar restaurant serves Mediterranean dishes, fresh fruit juices and a large selection of teas in its lovely interior garden (see p108).

- Map F2
- Ca'n Torró Library, Carrer d'en Serra, 15; 971 547311; May–Oct: 10am–2pm Tue–Sun, 5–8pm Tue–Fri; Nov–Apr: 10am–2pm Tue–Sun, 4–8pm Tue–Fri
- Sant Jaume Church, May–Oct: 10am–1pm Mon–Sat (to 3pm Tue); Mass: 8pm Tue–Sun (7:30pm winter), 9:30am, noon Sun; adm €1
- Museu Monogràfic, c/Sant Jaume, 30 (971 547004); 10am–4pm Tue–Fri, 10am–2pm Sat–Sun adm €3, includes adm to Pollentia Ruins
- Teatre Romà, C/de Sant Ana; open access; adm free

Top 10 Sights

1. City Walls
2. Historic Centre
3. Arab Quarter
4. Ajuntament
5. Ca'n Torró Library
6. Sant Jaume Church
7. Museu Monogràfic
8. Pollentia Ruins
9. Teatre Romà
10. Oratori de Sant Ana

City Walls

The walls were added after the Spanish conquest in the 14th century, with a second ring added in the 17th to further defend the town. By the 19th century they had begun to show the decrepitude of age and the vagaries of town and industrial expansion, but they have now been restored almost to their original state. They are pierced with gates and incorporate 26 towers in all.

Main gateway through city walls

Historic Centre

While modern Alcúdia extends beyond the city walls and has a commercial port town attached to it (see p41), most of the sights of historic interest are located within or near the walls. These include churches, mansions, a museum and some of the island's most significant Roman ruins.

Arab Quarter

The narrow streets of the old town (below) are resonant of what life must have been like under Arab rule, long after Roman orderliness had been buried. No one knows quite where the old souk (market) was, but it's easy to imagine artisan's shops, with their wares spilling out onto the dusty streets.

Ajuntament **4**
The handsome Mediterranean-Revival-style edifice was given its present look in 1929. Above the balcony is a grand tower with clock, belfry and weathervane, its pitched roofs gaily tiled in red and green stripes *(right)*.

5 Ca'n Torró Library
Opened in 1990, the library is housed in a prime example of aristocratic architecture in the 14th century. It hosts concerts and expositions.

6 Sant Jaume Church
The 14th-century church collapsed in the winter of 1870 but was recently rebuilt. The rose window is lovely, and the inner recesses feature amazing gold altars *(above)*.

7 Museu Monogràfic
Just one large room, but full of great finds, especially Roman artifacts and ceramics. Particularly intriguing are the beautiful bone pins and other implements for a Roman lady's toilette.

8 Pollentia Ruins
The Roman city *(left)* reached its peak in the 1st and 2nd centuries AD. You can see the foundations of what may have been the forum, and *insulae* (apartments). A few broken pillars have been propped up, but many of the stones have been removed over the centuries.

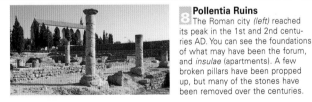

9 Teatre Romà
The island's only intact Roman theatre is also the smallest surviving one in Spain. Even so, it would have held about 2,000 people, and today is sometimes the venue for special concerts.

10 Oratori de Sant Ana
The tiny medieval chapel *(right)*, on the main road to Port d'Alcúdia, was built in the 13th century and features a stone carving of a very stocky Virgin and Child supported by an angel.

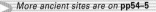
More ancient sites are on **pp54–5**

31

🔟 Coves del Drac

Known since ancient times, these limestone caves were mapped out by French geologist Edouard Martel in 1896. They are now one of Mallorca's top attractions. Hundreds of people at a time make their way along the cavernous path, where artfully lit rock formations and lakes conjure up marvellous

imagery. The name "Drac" means "dragon", probably in reference to the mythical creature's role as the fierce guardian of secret treasure.

Colourful rock formations

🟢 Allow time to stroll around the garden and visit the aquarium either before or after your tour of the grottoes.

🔵 A snack bar on-site sells sandwiches, olives and drinks. Otherwise, head to Porto Cristo for one of the terrace café-restaurants, such as S'Assecador *(see p118).*

• Map G4
• Coves del Drac, Porto Cristo (also sign-posted as "Cuevas del Drach" from down-town); 971 820753; 10am–5pm daily; tours once every hour except 1pm; adm €9.50 (free for under 7s)
• Acuàrio de Mallorca C/Gambí, Porto Cristo, 971 820971; 10:30am–6pm daily in summer, 11am–5:30pm in winter; adm €9.50 (free for children under 7)

Top 10 Features

1. Garden
2. Four Chambers
3. Formations
4. Lighting
5. Fanciful Figures
6. Subterranean Lakes
7. Performances
8. Boat Ride
9. Exit
10. Acuàrio de Mallorca

Four Chambers
Visitors descend to the caves through the Luis Armand Chamber, part of the Frenchman's Cave, which was discovered by Martel. The three other main caverns are called Black Cave, White Cave and Luis Salvador's Cave. The path is smooth and even, and no guide speaks, so that visitors have the opportunity to contemplate the scale and beauty of the place in peace.

Garden
As most visitors have to wait before their tour begins, the proprietors have thoughtfully created a beautiful garden by the entrance. Mediterranean trees and plants, such as olives, figs, violets and hibiscus provide the set-ting for striking displays of limestone – one piece even evokes the shape of a dragon. Gorgeous pea-cocks roam around.

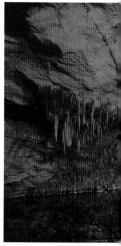

The subterranean Lake Martel

Formations
Thousands of stalactites (those hanging from above), stalagmites (those below), and columns (where the two meet) range from the finest needles to ponderous, mon-umental massifs *(left)*. There are also deep ravines, at the bottom of which you can see crystalline, impossibly aquamarine and turquoise pools.

Lighting
The cave illuminations are the work of engineer Carlos Buigas. Crevices, chasms, chasms, planes and spaces are highlighted to maximize the effects of *chiaroscuro* and depth *(right)*.

Fanciful Figures
Formations dubbed the "Inquisition Chamber" or "Ariadne's Labyrinth" were so named in the Middle Ages; the "Buddha" and "Flag" speak of more modern imaginations.

Subterranean Lakes
Of the several subterranean lakes here, Lake Martel is one of the world's largest, at 177 m (580 ft) long, with an average width of 30 m (98 ft). Its calm waters reflect the lighting effects of the performances *(entry 7)*.

Performances
Seated in an amphitheatre, in near pitch-darkness, the audience is regaled with a touching display at the end of the tour. Hypnotic lighting effects are accompanied by live music from a small chamber ensemble, floating by on a rowboat. Highlights include Albinoni's *Adagio*, Pachelbel's *Canon* and serene works by Bach, Handel, Chopin, Boccerini and others.

Exit
Visitors exit by foot past the Lake of the Grand Duchess of Tuscany and Chamber of the Columns to the Vestibule, which is a funnel-like tunnel leading back up to the surface.

Boat Ride
As a delightful climax to the performance, visitors are offered boat rides *(left)* on the lake – eight to a boat – steered by skilled gondoliers who employ an elegant figure-of-eight rowing style.

Acuario de Mallorca
A short walk from the caves brings you to a surprisingly good aquarium. The lower floor has scores of exotic species; the upper floor is devoted to denizens of the Mediterranean.

The Caves in Ancient Times

Large numbers of Talaiotic, Punic, Roman, Arab and Almoravid artifacts were discovered in the caves during archeological excavations in 1951. The finds are held in various museums around the island for safekeeping, but ruins of a Cyclopean corridor, indicating a prehistoric settlement, can still be seen at one point of Luis Salvador's Cave.

More ancient sites are on **pp54–5**

Left **Prehistoric walls** Centre **Christian sanctuary, Felanitx** Right **Alcúdia's post-Unification walls**

Moments in History

1 Prehistory
Neolithic pastoral societies have formed by at least 4000 BC. They live in the island's caves and keep domesticated animals. As bronze-working is introduced around 1400 BC, the Talayot period begins (see Ses Paisses and Capocorb Vell, p55).

2 Carthaginian Conquest
Various peoples, including the Greeks, use the island as a trading post. However, the absence of metal ores deters further colonization until the Carthaginian Empire spreads to this part of the Mediterranean in the 7th century BC.

3 Roman Conquest
In the third century BC, Carthage comes into conflict with the expanding Roman Empire. Rome is victorious in 146 BC and establishes order for the next 500 years. Roads and towns are built and, in AD 404, Mallorca and its neighbouring islands are established as the province of Balearica.

4 Vandal Invasion
No sooner is the new province officially recognized, however,

So-called Roman bridge, Pollença

than the Vandals sweep across the Balearics in about AD 425, swiftly ending Roman rule. So destructive is their takeover that few traces of the Romans are left.

5 Byzantine Conquest
In 533, the Byzantines defeat the Vandals and bring the Balearics under their rule, restoring prosperity and also an orthodox form of Christianity. From faraway Constantinople, Emperor Justinian rules the islands as part of the province of Sardinia. They enjoy this Byzantine connection until the end of the 7th century, then become more or less independent, with close ties to Catalonia.

6 Moorish Conquest
In 902, the Moors occupy the islands and turn them into a fiefdom of the Emirate of Córdoba. Through a succession of dynastic changes, they hold on for the next 327 years and forcibly convert all the inhabitants to Islam.

7 The Reconquista
In 1229, King Jaume I of Aragón rises to oppose the Balearic Moors. His forces first land on the western coast of the island at Santa Ponça, from where he marches eastwards to lay siege to Medina Mayurqa (the Moorish name for Palma). The city falls to him on 31 December, after three months.

Sign up for DK's email newsletter on traveldk.com

The 1479 marriage that unified Spain

8 The Kingdom of Mallorca
Despite Jaume's liberal treatment of islanders, and his laws embodied in the Carta de Població, the territory descends into turmoil after his death, due to rivalry between his sons. Eventually, his son Jaume II is restored and succeeded by his son Sanç and Sanç's nephew Jaume III.

9 Unification with Spain
In 1344 the islands are once again thrown into chaos when united with Aragón by Pedro IV. Jaume III is killed during a feeble attempt to retake his kingdom. In 1479, with the marriage of Fernando V of Aragón and Isabella I of Castile, Aragón is in turn absorbed into a new Spanish superstate. The islands become an outpost of little importance, ushering in centuries of decline.

10 Since 1945
Generalissimo Francisco Franco instigates the development of mass tourism, which brings a much-needed influx of foreign money. This transforms Mallorca from a backwater to one of the 21st century's choicest venues of international stardom.

Top 10 Historical Figures

1 Hannibal
The Carthaginian leader is said to have been born on the island of Cabrera, just off Mallorca (Ibiza and Malta also claim his birthplace).

2 Quintus Metellus
Roman Consul who occupied Mallorca and Menorca in the 2nd century.

3 Count Belisarius
Byzantine general who defeated the Vandals here in 533.

4 Emir Abd Allah
This Muslim leader conquered Mallorca and Menorca in the 10th century.

5 Jaume I
Christian king who took the islands back from the Moors in the 13th century and established remarkably liberal laws.

6 Pedro, Son of Jaume I
Jaume I's violent son Pedro and grandson Alfonso III tried to take Mallorca away from the rightful heir, Jaume II.

7 Jaume II
The rightful heir to Jaume I. He and his descendants carried on Jaume I's legacy until Mallorca was rejoined to the kingdom of Aragón.

8 Ramon Llull
Great 13th-century mystic, poet and scholar who had a profound influence on Mallorcan spiritual life.

9 Robert Graves
The 20th-century English writer, scholar and poet put Mallorca on the international literary map (see p96).

10 Adán Diehl
The Argentinean poet and visionary built the Grand Hotel Formentor in 1929 (see p29), marking out Mallorca as an upper-crust tourist destination.

For the Top 10 figures in religious history **see p53**

Left **Cap de Cala Figuera** Centre **Cap de Capdepera** Right **Parc Natural de S'Albufera**

Areas of Natural Beauty

1 Cap de Cala Figuera Peninsula

Marked by a lonely lighthouse, this undeveloped area is officially a military zone, but as long as it's not closed or guarded, you can walk out for a view of the entire bay. Nearby Portals Vells is another tranquil area, while Platja El Mago is a nudist beach. ◎ Map B5

2 Illa Dragonera

The spot that precipitated the current conservation movement on the island is a great place to hike, take a picnic or just visit for the sake of the cruise. In season, you can get a ferry at either Sant Elm or Port d'Andratx. ◎ Map A4

3 Mirador de Ricardo Roca

A chapel-like structure at this lookout point has "Todo por la patria" ("All for the Fatherland") over its door – a remnant from Fascist times – with "patria" blotched out some time ago by a liberal-thinking

member of the new Spain. From here and a nearby café you'll find dizzying views down to the sea far below. ◎ Map B3

4 Barranc de Biniaraix

Two pretty villages lie in a gorge opposite the towering presence of Puig Major, Mallorca's highest mountain. So evocative is the silence of the gorge – broken only by sheep's bells and the bleating of goats – that it has been sold as a record. ◎ Map C2

5 Gorg Blau

Created by seasonal torrents over millions of years, the ravine near Sóller and Puig Major is up to 400 m (1,312 ft) deep but only 30 m (98 ft) wide, with some sections never seeing daylight. Do not hike between the cliffs in winter *(see also p103)*. ◎ Map D2

6 Torrent de Pareis

A box canyon at the spot where the "Torrent of the Twins" meets the sea is one of the

Barranc de Biniaraix

In recent years, Mallorca has begun an active programme of preserving its natural habitats

Mountain reservoir in the Gorg Blau

great sights of the island. The scale of the scene, with its delicate formations and colours, is amazing, and the sense of solitude undisturbed, even by the usual crowds you will encounter here. The tunnel-like path from Cala Calobra was carved out in 1950. ◈ *Map D2*

Península de Formentor
This jagged spur of the great Serra de Tramuntana range has been saved from overdevelopment mostly due to the fact that a large luxury hotel was built here in the 1920s. The drive out to the lighthouse is unforgettable (*see pp28–9*). ◈ *Map F1*

Parc Natural de S'Albufera
Pliny wrote of night herons, probably from S'Albufera, being sent to Rome as a gastronomic delicacy. The wetlands were drained for agriculture in the 19th century. What land was left has now been restored and turned into a nature reserve – the Mediterranean's largest wetlands. ◈ *Map F2*

Cap de Capdepera
The island's easternmost point is a great place to hike around,

though the terrain generally necessitates little more than easy strolling. You can go out to the lighthouse on its cape of sheer rock, or check out the pristine coves that lie lined up to the north and south, including Cala Agulla, Son Moll, Sa Pedrusca and Sa Font de sa Cala. ◈ *Map H3*

Parc Natural de Mondragó
One of the newer preserves established on the island, this one is part nature, part heritage site. It incorporates a full range of island terrains, from wooded hills to sandy dunes, as well as an assortment of rural structures. Come here for hiking, bird-watching, picnicking, swimming or simply getting a feel for old Mallorca (*see p114*). ◈ *Map F6*

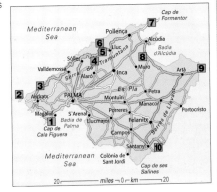

See Around the Island for resorts and other attractions close to these areas of natural beauty

Left **Balearic cyclamen** Right **S'Albufera wetlands**

⒑ Wildlife and Plants

1 Birds of Prey
The island's dashing Eleanora's falcons constitute an important part of the world's population – you can see them around the Formentor lighthouse *(see p29)*. The peregrine falcon, too, breeds in these parts, and you can spot black vultures, red kite, eagles, Montagu's harrier and long-eared owl.

2 Marine Birds
Birdwatchers come from all over Europe to see rare migrants, especially at the S'Albufera wetlands *(see p37)*, including marsh harriers, herons, egrets, stilts, bitterns and flamingos. Seagulls (including the rare Audouin's gull), sandpipers, cormorants, ducks, ospreys and terns live along the rocky coasts.

Wild goat

3 Songbirds
Species breeding here, or stopping for a visit in the spring or summer, include stonechats, warblers, the stripy hoopoe, partridges, buntings, finches, larks, curlews, thrushes, martins, ravens, shrikes, turtle doves, pipits,

Bee-eater

swifts, swallows, the brilliantly coloured European bee-eater and the inimitable nightingale.

4 Mammals
You should see plenty of wild mountain goats in the more remote areas of Mallorca – and they'll certainly spy you. Rabbits, hares, hedgehogs, civet cats, ferrets, weasels and other small creatures may take longer to spot. The Mallorcan donkey is also an increasingly rare occurrence – having been cross-bred with its Algerian cousin, there are a mere handful of registered members of the unalloyed species that exist at present.

5 Reptiles and Amphibians
Frogs, salamanders, geckos, snakes and lizards abound on the island. But perhaps the most interesting creatures are the endangered ferreret, a type of frog found only in the ravines of the Serra de Tramuntana, and the Lilford's lizard. Hunted to extinction by their natural enemies on the main island, the latter still thrive on the smaller islets off shore, especially Cabrera. Another endangered species is the caretta turtle, which lives in the waters around Sa Dragonera and Cabrera.

6 Insects
In the warmer seasons, you'll see plenty of colourful

Mallorca is one of the most important stopover points in the Mediterranean for migrating birds

butterflies in the wooded areas of the island, as well as bees, mayflies and mean-looking hornets. In hot weather, especially among cedars, you'll be treated to the song of the cicadas, keening away at full volume, a wonderful reminder that you're in the Mediterranean. But flies and mosquitoes might take some dealing with.

Orange groves, Serra de Tramuntana

7 Wildflowers

The island is home to over 1,300 varieties of flowering plants, of which 40 are uniquely Mallorcan. These include the Balearic cyclamen, giant orchids and the delicate bee orchid. Spring and early summer are the time to see them in all their colourful bounty, but autumn also can be good. Look out especially for the asphodel with its tall spikes and clusters of pink flowers, Illa de Cabrera's rare dragon arum with its exotically hairy look, the rock rose in the Serra de Tramuntana and the Balearic peonies.

8 Herbs and Shrubs

These include the hairlike wild grass (*Ampelodesma mauritanica*) used for fodder, thatching and rope; the Balearics' only native palm, the dwarf fan palm; giant yucca and aloe; palmetto, used for basketry; aromatic wild rosemary; wild broom; a native variety of St John's wort; and the giant fennel.

9 Trees

The mountain areas are characterized by pines, cedars and evergreen holm oaks, while palms, cypress and yews have been planted on the island since time immemorial. Olives can reach great age (more than 1,000 years) and gargantuan size. They can also take on disturbingly anthropomorphic forms – the 19th-century writer George Sand, in her book *A Winter in Majorca (see p18)*, tells of having to remind herself "that they are only trees", when walking past them at dusk.

10 Cultivated Plants

Some of the flowering plants you see around the island are actually cultivated for decorative purposes: for example, the oleander, purple morning glory, agapanthus, bougainvillea, *Bignonia jasminoides* (commonly called the trumpet vine, with both orange and pink blooms – used as cover for pergolas), geranium and wisteria. Grapes and olives have been a feature of the Mallorcan landscape since Roman times.

Wildflowers in spring

Left **Port de Pollença** Right **Port d'Alcúdia**

TOP 10# Ports and Resorts

1 Cala Fornells
A pleasant resort made up of coves with turquoise water, sandy beaches and large, flat rocks on which to bask. Families flock here, and it's good for snorkelling. Nearby Peguera has the nightlife (see p42). Map B4

Port de Sóller

2 Port d'Andratx
One of the choicest resort ports on the island, frequented by the Spanish king and other stellar visitors. Most of the restaurants and shops are on the south side of the port, with a posh sailing club on the north. The water is azure and lapis, with touches of emerald, but the only beach is tiny. Map A4

3 Port de Valldemossa
More a cove than a port, the beach here is rocky, the houses are made of rock, and rocky villas are dotted on the hill. Getting here involves a hair-raising series of hairpin bends down a cliff face that's subject to rockslides, especially after rains. The lone restaurant, Es Port, is a treat (see p100). Map C3

4 Cala Deià
A narrow winding road from Deià (see p96) leads to a picturesque cove surrounded by steep cliffs. The beach is shingle, and the water is very clear. Getting down to the car park is the usual routine of narrow switchbacks. Map C2

5 Port de Sóller
The lovely bay offers calm waters for swimming, and a

Port d'Andratx

Some of Mallorca's best ports have been developed as top resorts; others are still little more than quaint fishing villages

pedestrian walk lines the beaches. The resort hotels and nightlife venues cater to both young and old. Don't miss a ride on the antique tram that scoots to and from downtown Sóller *(see also p96)*. ◈ *Map C2*

Port de Pollença

The family-friendly resort situated 6 km (4 miles) to the east of Pollença town, beside a pleasant bay, is an attractive place with a long, sandy beach. Many retired foreigners have made the town their home *(see also p104)*. ◈ *Map E1*

Port d'Alcúdia

Big and a bit brash, this resort town has it all, including what most visitors might prefer to do without – terrible fast food joints and too many fluorescent lights creating a ghostly pallor along the promenade by night. Still, the beaches are good, some of the restaurants excellent and the nightlife non-stop *(see also p105)*. ◈ *Map F2*

Cala Rajada

Ideal for watersports of all kinds, but the town itself feels a little cramped and overused, though it is still a fully operational fishing port. Fine coves and beaches nearby include popular Cala Guyá, Cala Mezquida and Cala Torta, which allows nudists *(see also p116)*. ◈ *Map H3*

Platja de Canyamel

If a tranquil resort is what you're after, this might be the place to come. Even in high season, it remains a

quiet, family-oriented place – just a long, curving sandy beach backed by pine forests, with a few tasteful hotels here and there. ◈ *Map H3*

Portopetro

Although on the verge of being swallowed whole by Cala d'Or *(see also p116)*, this little fishing village has so far managed to retain its original flavour – possibly because there is no beach, and only one hotel in town. Charming to walk around and admire the slopes dotted by villas, or maybe just use as your base to vist the entire area. ◈ *Map F6*

Cala Rajada

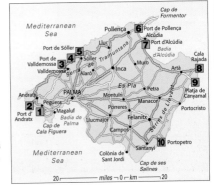

Left **Peguera** Right **Cala d'Or**

TOP 10 Beaches

1 Platja de Palma/S'Arenal
At the height of the holiday season, this 5-km (3-mile) long beach near the airport becomes exceptionally busy. Numerous hotels, apartments and clubs crowd behind a row of cafés and bars next to the beach. ◈ Map C4/T2

2 Peguera
A sprawling hotch-potch of modern structures and tourist attractions on a bay ringed by sandy beaches and pleasant pine forests. This is where Jaume I, the Conqueror, first came ashore with his army to retake the island from the Moors; now the only interlopers are the yachting enthusiasts in the ultramodern marina. ◈ Map B4

3 Camp de Mar
This tiny, modern *urbanització* (development) has an excellent beach and a pier running out to a small rocky island in the middle of the cove. You can also climb up on the windswept cliffs of Cap d'es Llamp. ◈ Map B4

Platja de Formentor

4 Cala Tuent
On the wild northern coast, where the opalescent hues of massive cliffs and sea meet, this is probably the area's quietest beach, since it's bypassed by most of the crowds who come to see the nearby Torrent de Pareis *(see pp36 & 103)*. ◈ Map D2

5 Cala Sant Vicenç
The area consists of three coves – Cala Sant Vicenç, Cala Barques and Cala Molins – with an appealing aura of intimacy. The first two have tiny but perfect beaches, gorgeous water and views. The third is down a hill, with a broader beach and more of a singles atmosphere *(see p104)*. ◈ Map E1

Camp de Mar

Cala Millor

Platja de Formentor

Daytrippers from Port de Pollença love to come here, either by car or ferry, to partake of the same pristine sands and pure waters as the guests of the grand Hotel Formentor. The unspoiled views here are among the very best on the island *(see also p29)*. ⊗ *Map F1*

Cala Millor

One of the most popular resorts on the east coast of Mallorca. The first hotels began to appear here as early as the 1930s, but the real tourist invasion did not start until the 1980s. Similar to neighbouring Cala Bona and Sa Coma, Cala Millor has many beautiful beaches; the main one is 1.8 km (1 mile) long and is quite magnificent. There are bars, restaurants and clubs aplenty, all over-crowded in summer. To see what this coast used to be like, walk to the headland at Punta de n'Amer nature reserve. ⊗ *Map G4*

Cala d'Or

Actually a collection of eight coves, which, taken together, comprise the most upmarket enclave on the southeastern coast. Though sprawling, the developments are characterized by attractive low-rise, white structures abundantly swathed in greenery *(see p116)*. ⊗ *Map F5*

Colònia de Sant Jordi

The town has a handful of modest hotels, a few restaurants, a pretty beach and an interesting harbour. Many people come here with the sole purpose of catching a boat to nearby Cabrera *(see p115)*, which, according to Pliny, was the birthplace of the famous Carthaginian leader, Hannibal. The town's other main attraction is the nearby salt lake, from which huge quantities of salt were once extracted – the main source of the town's wealth. ⊗ *Map E6*

Es Trenc

This splendid beach is everyone's favourite, and weekends will find it very crowded with sun-worshippers from Palma. The rest of the week, it's the domain of nudists, nature-lovers, and neo-hippies. It remains the island's last natural beach, interrupted only by the complex of vacation homes at Ses Covetes *(see p116)*. ⊗ *Map E6*

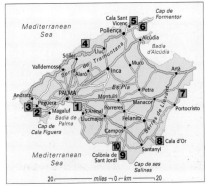

Left **Portals Vells** Right **Entrance to the Coves D'Arta**

Coves and Caves

1 Illetes
The western side of Palma Bay is generally upmarket, and "The Islets" typify the area's allure. Tiny islands, intimate coves, rocky cliffs and rolling hillsides are accentuated with attractive villas and a scattering of exclusive hotels. ☉ Map C4/R2

Ses Illetes

2 Portals Nous and Bendinat
These merged developments form one of the more exclusive resorts on the Bay of Palma: not many high-rise hotels, just rows of private villas and apartments dominating the shoreline. Port Portals marina is the summer home of the jet-set. ☉ Map C4/R2

3 Portals Vells
Near the southern tip of Palma Bay's western shore, several virtually private coves and their sandy beaches await, including

Bendinat

this one and adjacent Cala Mago, the only officially nudist beach near the city. The rocky cliffs are the stuff of local legend, which recounts that shipwrecked Italian sailors fulfilled a vow in recompense for their salvation by carving an entire chapel out of solid rock (see p58). ☉ Map B5/Q3

4 Coves de Gènova
Though they pale in comparison with the larger caverns on the eastern coast, these caves, discovered in 1906, are close to Palma and feature some interesting formations. A knowledgeable guide will show you around.
☉ C/Barranc, 45, Gènova • Map C4/R2
• 971 402387 • Jun–Sep: 10am–1:30pm & 4–7pm daily; Oct–May: 10:30am–1pm & 3–5:30pm Tue–Sun • Adm €8

5 Cala Pi
Lush and beautiful, with an immaculate beach and excellent restaurants. Perhaps because of the abundant vegetation, the air seems fresher here than elsewhere on the island. ☉ Map D6

Mallorca's coastline is characterized by countless coves, many of them beautiful and some of them with remarkable caves nearby

Rocky cove, Palma Bay

6 Cova Blava (Blue Grotto)

This pretty little waterside cave is incorporated as part of the return trip to the island of Cabrera (see p115). Like it's famous forerunner on the Isle of Capri in Italy, this Blue Grotto offers the amazing spectacle of the outside light being filtered up through the aquamarine waters, creating a ravishing luminosity that seems at once spectral, gem-like, and visually delicious. You can swim here, too. ◈ Map H6

7 Coves del Drac

Take a quiet walk through an underground fairyland. The visit incorporates a concert on the large underground lake, with captivating lights reflected in the mirror-like waters. Then take a boat to the other side and continue your exploration (see pp32–3). ◈ Map G4

8 Coves d'es Hams

The lighting in these caverns is more carnival-like than the others, and there's also a subterranean lake, with boat rides and a light and music show as part of your tour. Guides will give enough information to delight a speleologist, and the peculiar cave-dwelling crustaceans will be pointed out (see p113). ◈ Map G4

9 Coves d'Artà

These caves have inspired many over the centuries, especially since they were studied in the 19th century. In summer, you can take a boat cruise to them from Cala Rajada and Font de Sa Cala – the seaside exit is very dramatic (see p113). ◈ Map H3
• Cruises May–Oct: three daily

10 Cala Figuera, Cap de Formentor

Cutting a chunk out towards the very end of dramatic Península de Formentor, this cove lies at the bottom of a precipitous ravine. It's accessible either on foot – you park up above, just off the road that winds out to the lighthouse – or by boat. Once there, the views of the surrounding cliffs are awesome, and the beach and water make it one of the island's most inviting swimming spots (see p29). ◈ Map F1

Cala Figuera

Confusingly for English-speakers, caves are called **coves** in Mallorquin and Catalan, while coves are called **calas** in Spanish

Left **Cycling** Centre **Golf** Right **Paragliding**

Outdoor Activities and Sports

Watersports at Cala Deia

1 Snorkelling and Diving

Virtually all the tranquil coves around the island are ideal for snorkelling, with plenty of rocks and hidden recesses to explore. A favourite is the cove down from Estellencs *(see p50)*. As for scuba diving, there are several centres, including at Port d'Andratx and Cala Rajada *(see pp40–41)*, offering the gear and boat trips out to the best spots.

2 Other Watersports

Paragliding and jet-skiing are popular. Though windsurfing is also popular around the whole island, it is really best only on the eastern and southern coasts, where the waters tend to be calmer, and within the protected bay of the Port de Sóller *(see pp40 & 96)*. You can hire the equipment from various establishments along the beaches.

3 Hiking and Rock-Climbing

The island is a hiker's dream, with no end of trails, many of them marked and mapped out. There are compelling challenges for climbers, too, on the rocky cliffs that abound along the entire length of the Serra de Tramuntana, from Sóller in the west to the end of the Península de Formentor in the east. Tourist offices and parks offer published guidelines for tackling the island's wilds.

Climbing near Sóller

4 Cycling

You'll see groups of avid cyclists, decked out in their colourful threads, all over the island, from the twistiest mountain roads to the narrowest stone-walled lanes of Es Pla. Given the challenges most people experience when driving in Mallorca, it takes a bit of nerve to negotiate the same roads on two wheels. But you can easily rent bikes of all types in most towns, and the landscape is certainly conducive to cycling.

Watersports equipment for hire

5 Golf

This is a sport that has taken Mallorca by storm. Courses are prevalent near the big resorts, though some of the finer hotels have their own and many more have putting greens. There are some 18 major golf courses scattered all around the island.

Ⓢ Golf Son Termens, Bunyola (971 617862) • Capdepera Golf (971 818500) • Club de Golf Vall d'Or, Portocolom-Cala d'Or (971 837001)

6 Boating

You can hire sail boats or motor boats for yourself, or sign on for a full-day or sunset cruise, many of which also feature water-skiing and other activities, and buffet lunches. They are the only way to explore some of the island's more inaccessible – and therefore virtually private – coves.

7 Fishing

As with other water activities, there are a number of boats that will take you out fishing for the day, particularly from the small port towns that still fish the seas commercially, including Portocolom (see p116). The bays of Pollença and Alcúdia (see pp104–5) are also popular for fishing.

8 Bird-Watching

Nature reserves are best for bird sightings, especially those on the north-eastern coast, S'Albufera and the Península de Formentor (see pp36–7). Spring and autumn are optimal times to visit, when migratory birds use Mallorca as a staging post between Europe and Africa. The isolated islands of Sa Dragonera and Cabrera (see p115) are also excellent.

9 The Bullfight

There are five bullrings: in Palma, Muro, Alcúdia, Inca and Fulanito, though historically the bullfighting tradition has not been so important to Mallorcans (or to Catalans generally) as in other parts of Spain. In season, between March and October, there are eight or nine bullfights. The killing, albeit executed according to strictly ceremonious guidelines, can be bloody and pathetic, so be warned.

10 Fútbol

There are two football (soccer) teams in Mallorca: Real Mallorca and Atlético Baleares, both of whom play in Palma during the season, which runs from early September to April. Real Mallorca has enjoyed considerable success in recent years, and, in any case, attending a match can be a fun, high-spirited, and good-humoured way to see the locals participating in the game they love the best.

Yachts, Port d'Andratx

Left **Walkers, Palma** Centre **Bunyola–Orient road** Right **Sa Calobra road ("The Snake")**

🔟 Walks and Drives

Section of Palma's city walls

1 Palma's Walls (Walk)
The best part of the old wall for walking is along the Parc de la Mar *(see pp64 & 90)*. 🚶 *Map K–P5*

2 La Reserva (Walk)
The reserve on the slopes of Puig de Galatzó is best described as "Mallorca's paradise". A 3.5 km (2 mile) trail leads past waterfalls, springs and olive trees. 🚶 *Map B3 • Two hours • Adm €10.50*

3 Sant Elm to Sa Trapa (Walk)
This popular walk leads to an old Trappist monastery (and future mountain refuge) and has fine views of the island of Sa Dragonera. A shorter route is signposted beside the cemetery on the Sant Elm–Andratx road. 🚶 *Map A4 • Three hours for whole route*

4 Puig de Santa Eugènia (Walk)
From the village of Santa Eugènia, walk to Ses Coves, used at various times as bandit hideouts and wine cellars. From here, a series of tracks takes you up to a pass and the cross on the summit of Puig de Santa Eugènia, affording fine views. 🚶 *Map D3 • Two hours to top*

5 Archduke's Mulepath (Walk)
Only experienced walkers should attempt this day-long round trip from Valldemossa. Red markers take you up to a *mirador* and a high plateau before dropping back down through a wooded valley. 🚶 *Map C3 • Six hours*

6 Andratx Round Trip (Drive)
Take the main highway north of Andratx to the Mirador Ricardo Roca, Banyalbufar, then Mirador de ses Ànimes *(see p56)* for stunning perspectives. Turn towards Sa Granja, then pass down through Puigpunyent, Puig de Galatzo, Galilea, Es Capdellà and back to Andratx. 🚶 *Map B3–4 • Two hours*

7 Old Road to Sóller (Drive)
The drive over the Coll de Sóller, with its 57 hairpin bends, is the most terrifying in Mallorca. But it's worth it to see what life used to be like before the tunnel opened. 🚶 *Map C3 • About 45 minutes*

View from Sa Calobra

Since most of the island remains undeveloped, there are plenty of opportunities to explore off the beaten track

Mirador de ses Anímes

Sa Calobra (Drive)

8 Driving anywhere around Puig Major affords great views and challenges your driving skills. This purpose-made road – which translates as "The Snake" – has earned its name, with 270-degree loops and other harrowing features. It leads to a tiny settlement, where you can explore the dazzling beauties of the box canyon created over aeons by surging torrents *(see p106)*. ⓢ *Map D2 • About 30 minutes*

Pollença to Puig de Maria (Walk)

9 You'll find the signpost to Puig de Maria at Km 52 on the main road from Palma to Pollença. A sanctuary, set on an isolated hill that dominates the bays of Pollença and Alcúdia, offers stirring views of the Península de Formentor. ⓢ *Map E1–2 • 90 minutes to top*

Bunyola–Orient–Alaró (Drive)

10 Another extremely narrow road that threads its way along precipitous mountain ridges, but worth it for the unforgettable views. The town of Orient is a pretty eagle's-nest of a place, and the glimpse of Castell d'Alaró will fire your imagination *(see p50)*. ⓢ *Map C3–D3 • About 1 hour with stops*

Top 10 Peaks

1 **Puig Major**
The island's highest mountain is part of the Tramuntana range. Its stark, rocky prominence provides a powerful landmark for miles around *(see p106)*. ⓢ *1,447 m (4,747 ft)*

2 **Puig de Massanella**
The highest mountain that can actually be climbed on the island. ⓢ *1,367 m (4,484 ft)*

3 **Puig de ses Bassetes**
Southwest of Massanella, near the beautiful Gorg Blau reservoir, among some of Mallorca's most stirring landscapes. ⓢ *1,216 m (3,989 ft)*

4 **Puig d'es Teix**
In the heart of the most verdant part of the Tramuntana, northeast of Valldemossa. ⓢ *1,062 m (3,484 ft)*

5 **Puig Galatzó**
Overlooks the picturesque valley of Puigpunyent, north of Palma. ⓢ *1,025 m (3,363 ft)*

6 **Puig Roig**
Just north of the holy site of Lluc and named for its reddish colour ⓢ *1,002 m (3,287 ft)*

7 **Puig Caragoler**
Access is via Camí Vell de Lluc, a pilgrim trail that used to be the only way to get to Lluc Monastery. ⓢ *906 m (2,972 ft)*

8 **Puig Morell**
Good for hiking, this is the highest peak in the Serres de Llevant by the southeast coast. ⓢ *560 m (1,837 ft)*

9 **Puig de Randa**
The only highpoint on the Central Plain – site of Santuari de Nostra Senyora de Cura *(see p61)*. ⓢ *543 m (1,781 ft)*

10 **Puig Sant Salvador**
The second highest peak in the Serra de Llevant, home to a well-loved monastery *(see p61)*. ⓢ *510 m (1,673 ft)*

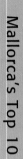

On mountain hikes, take food and water, a map, compass, whistle and mobile phone, as well as protection from sun, wind and rain

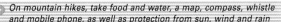

Left **Estellencs** Right **Capdepera**

🔟 Villages

1 Estellencs

Though it is a pretty terraced town in a magnificent mountain setting, its old houses of grey-brown stone – left unplastered and unadorned – were essentially built for defence. Even the 15th-century church belfry was used as a place of refuge, as were most towers on the island *(see also p98)*. ◈ Map B3

2 Deià

Spilling down a steep hillside, Deià's earth-tone houses are, to many, the finest on the island. English poet and writer Robert Graves and his artistic friends certainly thought so, bringing international fame to this really rather modest town. Today, the tiny artists' retreat has been bought up by the wealthy, though it still retains its humble appearance *(see also p96)*. ◈ Map C2

3 Fornalutx

Often voted Mallorca's loveliest town – if not all of Spain's – this enchanting mountain village was founded by the Moors in the 12th century. The tiny town square is a friendly gathering place, but it is the heady views people remember – up to the island's highest mountain and down into a verdant chasm below *(see also p97)*. ◈ Map D2

Fornalutx

4 Orient

Again, it is the mountain setting that dazzles: this tiny, remote hamlet of some 40 houses has some of the finest views the island has to offer. It's also an excellent base for hikers or anyone who just wants to breathe the exhilarating air *(see also p98)*. ◈ Map D3

5 Alaró

At one end of a very scenic mountain road, under the shadow of the commanding Castell d'Alaró, this pleasant village dates from at least the time of the Moors. If you want to climb up to the castle, drive up to Es Verger restaurant and proceed on foot: the ascent takes about 45 minutes and the view is marvellous *(see p97)*. ◈ Map D3

Alaró

Orient

Binissalem

The town is probably second only to Palma in the number and splendour of its mansions, dating from the 18th century, when it became the centre of a booming wine business. All that ended at the end of the 19th century, when phylloxera wiped out the vines, but wineries are making a comeback these days, producing good reds *(see p121)*. ⊗ *Map D3*

Santa Maria del Camí

A way station for weary travellers through the centuries, the village has a charming Baroque belfry, the Convent dels Mínims and a quaintly traditional Mallorcan textile factory *(see p124)*. ⊗ *Map D3*

Algaida

Most people pass through the outskirts of this small town on their way to Puig de Randa, but it's worth stopping for some good restaurants, where the people of Palma dine at weekends *(see p125)*. The Gordiola Glassworks *(see p123)*. are also nearby. ⊗ *Map D4*

Santanyí

Founded in 1300 by Jaume II, Santanyí was given a protective wall due to its proximity to the coast. Only part of that wall remains but it gives the place a certain character. For this reason, the town has attracted a large number of foreign dwellers, who have turned it into a rather cosmopolitan, well-kept place compared with nearby towns. Check out the art galleries on the main square *(see also p117)*. ⊗ *Map F6*

Capdepera

The extremely large and well-preserved medieval fortress that dominates the ridge above the town is the main reason to come to Capdepera. With its crenellated walls draped over the rolling hilltop, it is certainly a noble sight and one of Mallorca's finest castles. Some sort of fort has been here since at least Roman times, and more or less continuously used throughout centuries of international squabbles and pirate raids *(see also pp57 & 113)*. ⊗ *Map H3*

Watching the Setmana Santa procession in Palma

Festivals

1 Revetlla de Sant Antoni Abat

One of Mallorca's most unusual festivals, in honour of St Anthony, the patron saint of pets. For two days in January in Sa Pobla, pets are led through the town to be blessed outside the church. Elsewhere, dancers drive out costumed devils, to ensure harmony during the coming year, and everyone circles bonfires and eats spicy pastries filled with spinach and marsh eels. ◈ 17 Jan • Palma, Sa Pobla, Muro and elsewhere

Festa de Sant Jaume

2 Maundy Thursday

Setmana Santa (Holy Week) in the capital city is observed by a solemn procession of some 5,000 people parading an icon of the crucified Christ through the streets. ◈ Mar or Apr • Palma

3 Good Friday

Many Mallorcan towns have processions during Holy Week. The Calvari steps in Pollença are the scene of a moving re-enactment, the Davallament (the Lowering) each Good Friday, when in total silence a figure of Christ is removed from a cross and carried down the steps by torchlight. ◈ Mar or Apr • Pollença & elsewhere

4 Festes de Sant Sebastià

Mallorca's capital city honours its patron saint with fireworks, dragons, processions, street concerts and beach parties in one of the island's most colourful and exuberant festivals. ◈ last fortnight in January • Palma de Mallorca

5 Festa de Nostra Senyora de la Victòria

Port de Sóller is the venue for a mock battle between Christians and Moors, in commemoration of a skirmish in which Arabic corsairs were routed in 1561. Expect lots of rowdy, boozy fun, brandishing of swords and the firing of antique guns. ◈ Around 9 May • Port de Sóller

6 Corpus Christi

Participants dress up as eagles and perform the Ball dels Àguiles ("Dance of the Eagles") in Pollença's town square. What exactly this has to do with the miracle of Transubstantiation during Holy Communion is not really explained, thus scholars suspect the celebration's origins are pre-Christian. ◈ Jun • Pollença

7 Día de Mare de Déu del Carme

This celebration of the patron saint of seafarers and fishermen takes place in various coastal settlements. Boats are blessed, torches are lit (as at Port de Sóller), and sailors carry effigies of the Virgin. ◈ 15–16 Jul • Palma, Port de Sóller, Colònia de Sant Pere, Portocolom, Cala Rajada & other ports

Christians fighting Moors, Port de Sóller

8 Festa de Sant Jaume
St James is celebrated with the usual summer highjinks, including folk dancing, fireworks and parades, featuring an icon of the saint and various religious symbols. ◈ *Week leading up to 25 Jul • Alcúdia*

9 Mare de Déu dels Àngels
Another, even longer, battle between the Christians and the Moors, this time in Pollença. The town spends a whole year preparing for the event, in which hundreds of youths dress up. ◈ *2 Aug • Pollença*

10 Festa de l'Àngel
Villages across Mallorca celebrate the Feast Day of the Angel with a pilgrimage to their local shrine. The biggest event takes place in Palma's Castell de Bellver *(see pp12–13)* but the pilgrimage from Alaró *(see p50)* to its castle is also very colourful. ◈ *Sunday after Easter*

Revetlla de Sant Antoni Abat

Top 10 Figures in Religious History

1 Lluc
Legend recounts that over 700 years ago, an Arab boy named Lluc, recently converted to Christianity, discovered the effigy of the Madonna at Lluc *(see pp26–7)*.

2 Ramon Llull
The 13th-century mystic founded several religious observances on the island.

3 Knights Templar
A rich and powerful brotherhood of Christian military monks *(see p90)*.

4 Inquisition Judges
The hated Inquisition was introduced to the island in 1484 and led to the burning alive of at least 85 people between 1484 and 1512.

5 Xuetes
The name given to the Jews who were coerced by the Inquisition into converting to Catholicism.

6 Junípero Serra
Important 18th-century missionary, born in the town of Petra *(see p122)*.

7 Santa Catalina
The island's only home-grown saint, Santa Catalina Thomàs was born in the 1500s in Valldemossa *(see pp18–19)*.

8 Cardinal Despuig
The 18th-century cardinal developed the more opulent side of church life on the island *(see p95)*.

9 Bishop Campins
The driving force behind the renewal of the monastery at Lluc as a pilgrimage site.

10 Gaudí
Highly devout, the architect was responsible for the restoration of Mallorca Cathedral and other holy sites.

CATHARINA THOMAS

Most island festivals are religious in origin, but some celebrate famous victories, some food and others the arts

Left **Ses Paisses** Right **Palau de l'Almudaina** Right **Jardins d'Alfàbia**

Ancient Places

1 La Seu, Palma
The Romans had some sort of major building on the site of Mallorca's Cathedral, and it was graced with an important mosque under the Moors. The existing edifice shows the stylistic influences of both those and other cultures *(see pp8–9)*.

2 Palau de l'Almudaina, Palma
Many Moorish elements can still be appreciated in the old, rambling palace *(see pp10–11)*.

3 Banys Àrabs, Palma
These private baths probably belonged to a wealthy Moorish resident and, together with their gardens, have incredibly come down to us virtually intact.

Banys Árabs

However, closer examination reveals elements from even earlier sources. The columns, each one different, were doubtlessly taken from an ancient Roman building *(see p87)*.

4 Jardins d'Alfàbia
Although later Renaissance and Baroque touches are evident in the gardens and house, the underlying Arabic styling predominates. The many watercourses are a distinctly Moorish touch, as well as the little oasis-like groves of trees encircling pools, where you can sit and enjoy the fresh air and the music of gurgling rivulets *(see pp24–5)*.

5 Castell d'Alaró
This lofty castle was originally used by the Moors as a stronghold. It proved to be virtually impregnable – conquered only after extremely long sieges, with its unfortunate defenders eventually being starved out. The Christians refurbished the old structure and continued to use it for centuries *(see p97)*.

6 Castell del Rei
The Moors chose another picturesque spot for their "Castle of the King". The battered ruins we see today, high above the sea on a barren crag, are the remains of medieval embellishments made by Jaume I. It was not effective against pirates, who simply landed at nearby Cala Sant Vicenç, but it was the last

Humans have inhabited Mallorca for at least 5,000 years – see pp34–5

stronghold to surrender to Aragonese invasions in the 14th century *(see p106)*.

7 Pollentia

The Moorish town of Alcúdia is built over an ancient Roman settlement called Pollentia. Little more than a few original Roman columns and foundations remain in situ – after being burned by Vandals in AD 440, the antique structures were dismantled to help create the new town *(see pp30–31)*.

Capocorb Vell

8 Ses Païsses

These Bronze Age remains form one of Mallorca's most impressive prehistoric sites. The defensive wall, composed of huge square blocks, is an example of the Mediterranean Cyclopean style – so-named by later cultures who believed that only a giant like the Cyclops could have built such a structure *(see p113)*.

9 Ses Covetes

Midway along the beach at Es Trénc is the site of what were probably ancient Roman burial grounds, where ashes of the dead were placed in small niches. It is called a *columbarium* (dovecote) because it resembles a pigeon house, with small openings lined up in rows *(see p116)*.

10 Capocorb Vell

These well-preserved megalithic ruins, from the Talaiotic culture that dominated the island some 3,000 years ago, are similar to those found at Ses Païsses. The word "Talayot" refers to the towers at such sites, which were two or three storeys high. The central round towers are the oldest elements here; around them is an encircling wall and square towers to complete the defensive complex *(see p115)*.

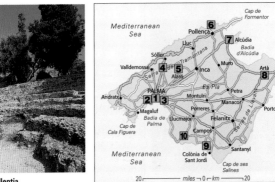
Pollentia

Left **Castell de Bellver** Right **Talaia d'Albercutx**

🔟 Castles and Towers

Castell de Bellver
1 One of just a handful of round castles in the world, and impeccably preserved, this building conjures up images of damsels in distress and bold knights galloping to the rescue. In fact, its history is more prosaic – it was a prison for enemies of the crown for hundreds of years *(see pp12–13)*.

Dragonera Island Tower
2 The ancient watchtower on one of Mallorca's most pictur-esque island nature reserves may date as far back as Roman times. It may not be much to look at these days, but it's fun just to hike around the unspoiled island and imagine what it must have been like during a raid, with corsairs storming the place and signal fires warning the rest of the island *(see p98)*.

Torre Verger at the Mirador de ses Anímes

Torre Verger
3 At the Mirador de ses Anímes, a watchtower, built in 1579, provides what must be among the finest views of the entire western coastline. You can climb up into the stone structure and stand on the topmost level, just as watchmen must have done in the dark centuries when Mallorca was subject to almost incessant attack by North African brigands *(see also p98)*.

Castell d'Alaró
4 This remote castle was attacked several times over the centuries, each time proving its defences against everything ex-cept prolonged siege. Alfonso III finally took it in 1285. The two leaders of the patriots were burned alive by the king, who, in turn, was excommunicated by the pope *(see also pp54 & 97)*.

Castell del Rei
5 With Moorish origins and Christian additions, this castle never served its defensive purpose well, as raiders simply avoided it. It was demoted to merely a watchtower, and, in the early 18th century, abandoned altogether. Today, its ruins are a panoramic destination for hikers *(see also pp54 & 106)*.

Talaia d'Albercutx
6 At the highest point on the Península de Formentor is a tower that is wondrous for having been built at all in such a precipitous

place. At this height, the wind howls, and the views are like those from a helicopter. The road to it is perilous, too *(see p28)*.

Sant Joan Baptista Belfry

Located in the town of Muro, this beautiful bell tower seems almost Arabic, so slender is the arch that joins it to the imposing church. However, it sports other

Santuari de Sant Salvador

elements that recall Gothic and Renaissance styles, including stone carvings, a decorative door and coffers. The square in which it is situated is one of the island's prettiest *(see p121)*.

Castell de Capdepera

Another wonderful Mallorcan fortress that epitomizes the fairy-tale castle. The approach is a pleasure in itself, as you pass fragrant plants and rocky outcrops, and the views are memorable. It was built by King Sanç in the 14th century *(see p113)*.

Castell de Santueri

One of several castles with the same name, this is about 6 km (4 miles) southeast of Felanitx. It was built in the 14th century right into the cliffs on the site of a ruined Arab fortress. The view takes in everything from Cabrera to the Cap de Formentor. You can drive here or walk, ideally from the equally imposing, nearby Santuari de Sant Salvador *(see p61)*.

Castell de Cabrera

The 14th-century castle on the island of Cabrera, off Mallorca's south coast, has a chequered history, subsequent to its original purpose as a defence measure for the southern reaches of the main island. At various times it has been a pirates' den; a crowded, deadly prison for 9,000 French soldiers in the 19th century; and an outpost for Franco's Fascist forces in the 20th century. Now the island it oversees is a National Park, and a climb up to the crumbling old fortress will be rewarded with some stupendous views *(see also p115)*.

Castell de Capdepera

Left **Portals Vells Cave Church** Centre **Sineu parish church** Right **Detail, Porreres hilltop church**

🔟 Churches

1 La Seu, Palma

Mallorca's grandest church is also one of the greatest Gothic churches anywhere. Flamboyant spires with stone flames give it a prickly look. The vast space and riches inside are also unforgettable *(see pp8–9)*.

2 Església de Santa Eulàlia, Palma

Built just after the Christians reclaimed the Balearics in the 13th century, this church has a rare Gothic homogeneity, despite some later medieval touches and 19th-century additions *(see p90)*.

3 Basílica de Sant Francesc, Palma

Built in 1281 on a site where the Moors made soap, this church has suffered its share of woes,

Interior, Santa Eulalia

Basílica of Sant Francesc

most notably when struck by lightning in 1580. Consequently, the façade you see today is a Baroque creation, though presumably no less massive than the Gothic original. The beautiful cloisters are the star turn, and, in fact, you must enter the church by going through them first *(see p88)*.

4 Portals Vells Cave Church

One of the caves along the rocky headland of Portals Vells *(see p44)* has been turned into a church, Cova de la Mare de Déu – according to legend, by shipwrecked Genoese sailors who were grateful for their survival. The holy water stoup and altar have been carved out of solid rock, although the effigy of the Virgin that was once placed here is now in a seafront church at Portals Nous.

5 Nostra Senyora dels Àngels, Pollença

Features include a vibrant rose window with elaborate arab-esque stone tracery outside and an intriguing sculpture, located in a side chapel, of St Sebastian, nonchalantly resting on the arrows that pierce his body. Note the floor tiles with rooster heads, the symbol of the town of Pollença *(see p103)*.

Every little village in Mallorca has a huge parish church dominating its central square

Nostra Senyora dels Àngels, Pollença

Santuari de la Victòria

The fortress church was built on a rocky headland near Alcúdia in the 1600s to house an early statue of the Virgin. Despite these measures, the figure was stolen twice by pirates. The views are sweeping, and it's also a starting point for great hikes over the promontory *(see p106)*.

Nostra Senyora de la Esperança, Capdepera

The story goes that once, when a band of loutish brigands were preparing to attack the town of Capdepera, the townspeople implored the Madonna to help them. A thick fog promptly settled in, confounding the pirates. Since then, the town's statue has been known as Sa Esperança ("the bringer of hope"). It is housed in a quaint Gothic chapel within the famous castle at Capdepera *(see p113)*.

Nostra Senyora dels Àngels, Sineu

Mallorca's grandest parish church, at the highest point of a town that was declared the official centre of the island by King Sanç, can be visited only on market day, Wednesday. It has a small archaeological museum. ✆ *Map E3*

Sant Bernat, Petra

Petra was the birthplace of Fray Junípero Serra, who established missions all over California in the 1700s and early 1800s. The town's stocky church commemorates the man *(see p122)*.

Oratori de Montesió, Porreres

Part of a former monastery, this 14th-century hilltop church overlooks the small agricultural village of Porreres. It has a five-sided cloister, an unusual arcaded façade with elegant Gothic lines, and great views out to sea. The setting is a wonderful venue for special concerts sponsored by the town, featuring internationally known talents. ✆ *Map E4*

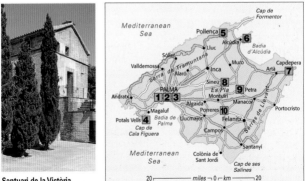

Santuari de la Victòria

Many churches on the island are open only for services; those with visiting hours generally open their doors 9am–noon & 4–6pm

59

Left **Carthusian Monastery** Right **Nostra Senyora de Lluc**

Monasteries

1 Carthusian Monastery, Valldemossa

Set in one of the most appealing towns on the island, this former royal residence and monastery has a rich history. Most captivating of all to the myriad visitors who come here is the poignant story of the winter visit of composer Frédéric Chopin, dying of tuberculosis, and his lover George Sand, along with her two children – all of whom left copious records of their experiences *(see pp18–19)*.

2 Ermita de Sant Llorenç

At Cala Tuent on the wild northern coast *(see p103)* is a small 13th-century hermitage perched high above the coast. It was remote then and remains relatively so today. ® Map D2

3 Nostra Senyora de Lluc

Not so much an active monastery today as a place of pilgrimage that also draws tourists and nature-lovers. This is Mallorca's holiest spot, high in the mountains, and has been a sacred zone since time immemorial. The complex has an attractive church, with a special chapel to house the venerated image, and there are also pilgrim paths to climb and nature trails to explore *(see pp26–7 & 146)*.

Ermita de Betlé

4 Ermita de Nostra Senyora del Puig

Just to the south of Pollença, this serene place with marvellous views houses one of the oldest Gothic images of the Virgin on the island. The unassuming stone complex, dating mostly to the 18th century, comprises a courtyard, a chapel, fortified walls, a refectory and cells. You can rent a room here *(see pp104 & 146)*.

5 Ermita de Betlem

Up in the hills northwest of Artà *(see p116)*, this monastery has a lovely vantage point, 400 m (1,312 ft) above the sea. It dates from 1804, when a group of hermits decided to rebuild the church that had been destroyed years before by pirates. The church is tiny and crudely frescoed, but it's worth the hike. Bring a picnic. ® Map G3

Ermita de Sant Miquel

Very few of the many monasteries actually have monks or nuns now, but most can be visited and have great views

6 Santuari de Sant Salvador

Pilgrims and other visitors can stay overnight at this former monastery, which has a truly spectacular setting, right at the top of the Serres de Llevant. You can't miss it: the site's huge stone cross and statue of Christ can be seen for miles around *(see pp114 & 146)*.

Santuari de Nostra Senyora de Cura

7 Ermita de Nostra Senyora de Bonany

This monastery is on top of Puig de Bonany. A stone cross was erected here in 1749 for Junípero Serra *(see p122)*, before he left on a mission to California. The sanctuary was built in the 17th century as an act of thanksgiving for a good harvest – *bon any* or "good year". The modern church dates from 1925 and is entered via an imposing gate decorated with ceramic portraits of St Paul and St Anthony. The forecourt has panoramic views. ✎ *Map F4*

8 Ermita de Sant Miquel

Just east of Montuïri *(see p123)* is a small monastery with views over the fertile fields of Es Pla. Facilities include a café-restaurant and nicely restored monks' cells where, for a nominal amount, you can stay so long as you don't mind sharing a bathroom. ✎ *Map E4*

9 Santuari de Nostra Senyora de Cura

Ramon Llull *(see p35)* founded this hermitage at the top of the Puig de Randa table mountain in the 13th century, and it was here that he trained missionaries bound for Africa and Asia. Nothing remains of the original building, but Llull's legacy has ensured that the site is an important place for many Catholics. The monastery houses a library and study centre, and visitors can stay overnight in simple rooms. There are other hermitages lower down the hill *(see next entry)*. ✎ *Map E4*

10 Santuari de Nostra Senyora de Gràcia

The lowest hermitage site on Puig de Randa *(see previous entry)* is set on a ledge in a cliff above a sheer 200-m (656-ft) drop and has beguiling views out over the plain. It was founded in 1497 and appears, along with nesting birds, to be sheltered by the huge rock that overhangs it. ✎ *Map E4*

Left **Museu Diocesà** Centre **Fundació Pilar i Joan Miró** Right **Spearheads, Museu de Mallorca**

🔟 Museums

1 Museu Diocesà, Palma

Housed in the former Episcopal Palace, this treasure trove contains archaeological artifacts, ceramics, coins, books and paintings spanning the 13th to 16th centuries. Highlights include the jasper sarcophagus of Jaume II, an

Museu d'Art Espanyol Contemporani

Arab tombstone and a painting of St George and the Dragon with a background impression of what 15th-century Palma might have looked like *(see p87)*.

2 Museu de Mallorca, Palma

The palace that houses this terrific museum dates from 1634. The collections present a full and well-documented range

Panel, Museu de Mallorca

of Mallorcan artifacts, from the prehistoric up to fine examples of Modernista furniture. The Talayot figures – small bronze warriors – and recreations of Neolithic dwellings are other highlights *(see p88)*.

3 Museu d'Art Espanyol Contemporani, Palma

One of the finer legacies left by Mallorcan Joan March, who became the world's third-richest man during the Franco era, in what many say was a dubious rags-to-riches rise. The renovated museum aims to spotlight the contributions of Spanish artists to the global art scene, so you'll find works by Picasso, Miró, Dalí and Gris, and also Mallorca's greatest modern painter, Miquel Barceló *(see p90)*.

4 Fundació Pilar i Joan Miró, Palma

Miró's Mallorcan roots go deep – both his mother and his wife were Mallorcan-born, and the great artist spent the last years of his life on the island. So it is

The style Catalans call Modernista is what some other countries call Art Nouveau, Liberty or Jugendstil

entirely fitting that the place he worked in that final period should have been turned into a museum devoted to him (see pp14–15).

Fundació Pilar i Joan Miró

Museu Municipal de Valldemossa
The range of objects on display is vast and eclectic, such as the history of printing in Mallorca, the work of an Austrian archduke, paintings inspired by the mountains of the Tramuntana, and important works by modern masters (see pp20–21).

Museu de Lluc
An interesting hotchpotch of prehistoric artifacts, Roman finds, ceramics (including some lovely majolica), religious pieces, and an exhaustive array of works by 20th-century Valdemossan artist Josep Coll Bardolet, who liked mountain scenery (see p27).

Museu Municipal de Pollença
In a former Dominican convent, the museum includes prehistoric sculptures shaped like bulls and an exquisite Tibetan sand painting given by the Dalai Lama in 1990.
🇸 C/Guillen Cifre de Colonya • Closed Mon • Adm

Museu Monogràfic, Alcúdia
This small but beautifully designed museum houses all the finds from ancient Roman Pollentia, such as cult figures, weights and measures, surgical instruments, needles, games, jewellery and gladiatorial gear (see p31).

Museu Etnològic, Muro
Fascinating glimpses into Mallorca's past include a recreated traditional kitchen pharmacy. There is a fine collection of *siurells* (Mallorcan clay whistles) featuring men on horseback. The Felanitx pottery bears the characteristic floral decoration. 🇸 C/Major, 15 • Map E3 • Closed Mon • Adm

Museu Gordiola
A fine exhibition of how Mallorcan glass is made and a museum dedicated to the history of glassmaking, from ancient Mesopotamia to the very latest high-style creations of the Murano works in Italy or Steuben in the US (see p123).

Glass, Gordiola

Museums tend to open around 10am, close at 1pm for a few hours, then reopen from around 5–7pm. They usually close on Mondays.

63

Left **Decorative wall at Parc de la Mar** Right **Jardines de Sa Faixina**

🔟 Parks and Gardens

1 Parc de la Mar, Palma
With its artificial lake, section of city walls and great views, this is a lovely place to stroll at any time. At night, the sparkling city lights and warm glow of the nearby cathedral and palaces add a magical quality *(see pp48 & 90)*.

2 S'Hort del Rei, Palma
Gentle jets of water and bowl-shaped fonts characterize this lovely Arab-influenced garden. As the name suggests, it was once the king's private garden. Today, it is open to all, and the home of some eccentric modern sculpture. ◈ *Map K4*

3 Banys Àrabs Gardens, Palma
To the Moors, who came from an arid land where the oasis was the symbol of life, water was the very essence of a garden. The cloistered gardens at the Banys Àrabs baths *(see p87)* evoke that ideal – it was here that the wealthy owner would relax after his bath, and breathe in the fragrant air.
◈ *Map M5 • Adm*

4 Jardines de Sa Faixina, Palma
These gardens start where Avinguda Argentina meets the Avinguda de Gabriel Roca, and run up to Plaça La Faixina alongside the old moat. The terraced

Jardins d'Alfàbia

lawns, fragrant trees and flowers and attractive fountains and columns provide a welcome respite from all the stone and asphalt of the newer sections of Palma. ◈ *Map J2*

5 Son Marroig
The famous Archduke Salvador *(see p20)* had many homes on Mallorca, but Son Marroig was his favourite. The gardens, terraced in the ancient Arabic fashion, are deliberately left a bit wild, in keeping with the slightly rough look of the natural flora. All this vibrant nature neatly contrasts with the high Renaissance refinement of the architecture, especially the gazebo that offers coastal views of such exquisite perfection *(see p95)*.

Banys Àrabs Gardens

Jardí Botànic

The botanical garden was founded in 1985 as a centre for the conservation and study of Mediterranean flora, especially that of the Balearics. The plants, many of which are endangered, include wild flora, medicinal herbs and flowers, fruit trees and vegetables. ⚲ *Ctra. Palma-Sóller, km 30.5, Sóller • Map C2 • 10am–6pm Tue–Sat, 10am–2pm Sun*

Jardins d'Alfàbia

The island's finest example of a profoundly Arabic garden dates back 1,000 years. Naturally, in all those centuries the lucky owners (Mallorca's most illustrious families among them) have added their own touches, resulting in Renaissance and Baroque elements in the landscape design and building features *(see pp24–5)*.

Raixa

Squarely of the late Italian Baroque or early Rococo style of the 1700s, Raixa gardens belonged to a wealthy cardinal, who liberally indulged his taste for collecting Classical statuary. However, only a fraction of his collection remains in the gardens; the rest now adorns the Castell de Bellver in Palma *(see pp12–13)*. ⚲ *Map C3*

Jardins Casa March (Sa Vall)

Joan March was a native-born magnate who allegedly made his fortune from illegal tobacco and arms trafficking. His old mansion near Cala Rajada, built in 1916, has lavish grounds incorporating water gardens, pine woods and fruit groves. Over

Son Marroig

40 works of modern sculpture in the gardens include a bronze by Rodin and a piece by Henry Moore. ⚲ *Map H3 • Visits arranged by the Tourist Office • 971 563033 • Adm*

Botanicactus

Europe's largest botanical garden has an amazing 12,000 cacti to admire, including a 300-year-old giant from Arizona. There are also the Balearics' largest navigable lake, palms and bamboo groves. Mallorcan flora is showcased through olives, pomegranates, almonds, pines, oranges, carobs and cypresses. ⚲ *Ctra. de Ses Salines a Santanyí, Ses Salines • Map E6 • 971 649494 • Apr–Sep: 9am–7pm; Oct–Mar: 10:30am–5pm • Adm*

Left **Marineland** Right **Coves d'Arta**

TOP 10 Family Attractions

1 Marineland
Children love the displays of dolphins, seals and sea lions showing off their acrobatic and aquatic skills. Kids can also swim in a pool of gentle rays, which feel like velvety gelatine. ◈ *Costa d'en Blanes, Calviá • Map Q2 • 971 675125 • mid-Feb–Oct: 9:30am–4:30pm • Adm*

2 Aqualand Magaluf
An extensive complex of pools and water slides to keep kids happy for a full day. Parents can relax in the garden areas. ◈ *Ctra. Cala Figuera, Magaluf-Calviá • Map Q2 • 971 130811 • Jun: 10am–5pm; Jul–Aug: 10am–6pm • Adm*

3 Western Park
The full title of this attraction is the "Western Park Crazy Wet West". Highlights include horse-riding shows, cowboys-and-Indians battles and can-can dancers. A water-park features water rides and chutes for the kids, and Jacuzzis for the grown-ups. Tots and teens both will love it, and mums and dads can relax in the garden-café areas between shows. ◈ *Ctra. Cala Figuera-Sa Porassa, Magaluf • Map B4/Q2 • 971 131203 • May, Jun & Sep: 10am–5pm; Jul & Aug: 10am–6pm • Adm*

4 Aqualand Arenal
Pools, slides and chutes galore at this huge water-park. Dragonland involves a giant sea-dragon whose mouth you can "ride". Other highlights include the Grand Canyon scoop slide and the Devil's Tail tube. There's also a great pool for kids. ◈ *Autovía Palma-Arenal, Km 15, salida (exit) 13 • Map T3 • 971 440000 • May–Oct: 10am–5pm; Jul & Aug: 10am–6pm • Adm*

5 Tram from Sóller to Port de Sóller
Board a tram at the little station above the main square of Sóller, which will take your family 5 km (3 miles) down through town and along the water's edge to the Port de Sóller. The cars are ex-San Francisco rolling stock from the 1930s, operating at a rattling snail's pace. ◈ *Map C2 • 7am–9pm; departs every half hour • Adm*

6 Museu de la Jugueta
Can Planes, a refurbished mansion in Sa Pobla, has a great

Aqualand Arenal

Sóller tram

Toy Museum with many Spanish antiques. Old comic strips, a doll that spins a hula-hoop around her waist, game boards and elaborate dolls' houses are some of the exhibits that will fascinate and delight the entire family. ⊗ C/Antoni Maura, 6, Sa Pobla • Map E2 • 971 542389 • 10am–2pm & 4–8pm Tue–Sat; 10am–2pm Sun • Adm

Hidropark

There's more than enough here to keep your brood busy for two full days. The water-park has one of the highest undulating slides on the island and the spiral tube satisfies the most demanding of thrill-seekers. For more sedate moments, you can play a round on the miniature golf course ⊗ Avda. Tucán, Port d'Alcúdia • Map F2 • 971 891672
• www.hidropark.com
• May–Oct: 10:30am–6pm (closed Sun in Oct) • Adm

Caves

Young adventurers will love the thrill of exploring Mallorca's caves, especially the Coves d'Artà, which exit onto the open sea (see pp44–5 & 113). At the Coves del Drac, the pitch darkness at a certain moment will excite your children, though

the very young might be frustrated at having to walk in silence for so long (see pp32–3).

Aqualandia

This small but lively park is situated away from the coast in the El Pla region (see pp120–25). Aqualandia has many attractions, including a water park with slides, a crazy golf course, and a wax museum. ⊗ Crta. Palma-Inca Km 25, Binissalem • 971 551228 • May–Sep: 10am–6pm • Adm

Jumaica

The Ca'n Pep Noguera is a banana plantation, which was established in 1973, when the owners started to transform the arid land into a tropical garden. It is a mini-paradise of farm animals, birds and exotic plants. ⊗ Ctra. Portocolom-Porto Cristo, Km 4.5 • Map G4 • 971 833979 • 9am–5:30pm daily • Adm

Western Park

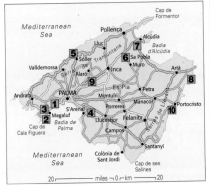

Tips for families are on **p134**

Left **El Corte Inglés** Right **Loewe fashion shop on Avinguda Jaume III**

🔟 Shopping Places

1 El Corte Inglés, Palma

Palma has two branches of Spain's only true department store, the quality and prices of which are firmly upmarket. ✪ *Avda. Alexandre Rosselló, 12 • Avda. Jaume III, 15 • 10am–10pm*

Avinguda Jaume III

2 Avinguda Jaume III, Palma

This elegant, arcaded avenue is one of Palma's main streets for chic boutiques, including Cartier and Loewe and good local shops such as Persepolis for antiques *(see p91)*. Worth a stroll even if you don't want to buy. ✪ *Map J–K2*

3 Casal Balaguer, Palma

A Renaissance-style 18th-century mansion is the showplace for local artists sponsored by the Círculo de Bellas Artes. ✪ *C/Unió, 3, Palma • Map M2 • 971 712489 • 11am–1:30pm, 5:30–8:30pm Tue–Fri, 11am–1:30pm Sat • Free*

4 Passeig de la Rambla, Palma

Built on what was once a seasonal river bed, this long promenade doesn't hold a candle to Barcelona's famous Ramblas, but is lined with flower stalls and definitely worth a ramble. ✪ *Map L1–M2*

5 Tejidos Artesania, Santa Maria del Camí

Wherever you go all over the island, you'll see the festive *robes de llengües* (tongue of flame cloth) they make here, in every possible colour and design. To watch it being made at this out-of-the-way spot is worth the trip in itself, plus you can buy bolts of fabric and ready-made items *(see p124)*.

6 Inca

Though Inca is a dull town, it is the island's centre for the production of leather goods. Countless outlets offer buttery leather jackets, supple handbags, trendy shoes and a host of other stylish items *(see p124)*.

7 Sa Pobla Market

The town's central square on a Sunday morning is the place to be if you want to see what a real

Flower stall, Passeig de la Rambla

For the best individual shops in Palma and around the island see pp91, 99, 107, 117 & 124. For shopping tips see p138.

Market stalls, Inca

country market is like. You will find the freshest produce – strawberries and potatoes are specialities here – and have the chance to sample the local spicy tapas *(see also p121)*.

Sineu Market

Sineu is one of the most interesting towns of Mallorca's central plain (Es Pla), and its Wednesday market is one of the biggest agricultural fairs in Mallorca, where local produce and livestock are traded. Pearls, leather and lace are among the goods on offer. ◈ *Map E3*

Manacor Pearls

The unprepossessing town of Manacor is notable for its manufactured goods, with pride of place going to its world-famous artificial pearls. The standards of fabrication are exacting, as a free tour of the factory will reveal, and the shimmering colours and variety of shapes indistinguishable from true pearls *(see also pp122 & 124)*.

Gordiola Glassworks

Despite the rather kitsch building it's housed in, this place is worth a prolonged visit. Watch the glassblowers engaged in their dangerous art, spend an hour in the museum upstairs, and at least another hour browsing through the vast warehouse shops with their prodigious output of beautiful glassware *(see p123)*.

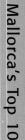

Top 10 Markets

Palma Daily Markets
Passeig de la Rambla for flowers *(see entry 4)*, Plaça Mayor, Mercado del Olivar, Mercado de Santa Catalina, Mercado de Pere Garau and Mercat de Llevant for produce.

Palma Weekly Markets
Sundays offer the huge Consell Market, while Saturday is the day for the vast El Rastro Palmesano Flea Market, on Avda. Alomar Villalonga.

Villages on Sunday
A great day for village markets: Valdemossa, Santa Maria del Camí, Inca, Sa Pobla, Pollença, Muro, Alcúdia, Portocristo, Portocolom, Felanitx and Llucmajor.

Villages on Monday
Manacor and Montuïri, also at Caimari, Calvia and Lloret.

Villages on Tuesday
Some of the lesser-known villages: Escorca, Campanet, Alcúdia, Santa Margalida, Artà, Portocolom, Porreres, S'Arenal.

Villages on Wednesday
Big day for markets, especially at Sineu. Others at Andratx, Escorca, Selva, Port de Pollença, Capdepera, Petra, Santanyí, Colònia de Sant Jordi and Llucmajor.

Villages on Thursday
The island's leather capital, Inca, as well as Escorca, Campos, Ses Salines, Llucmajor.

Villages on Friday Morning
Inca for leather, Binissalem, for wine, and Esporles, Escorca, Son Severa, Marratxi and Algaida.

Villages on Friday Afternoon
Alaró and Can Picafort.

Villages on Saturday
Naturally, Saturday is a big market day all over the island.

All markets normally run from very early in the morning until about 2pm, except for the two Friday afternoon markets noted

Left **Abraxas dance floor** Centre **Tito's logo** Right **Gran Casino Mallorca entrance**

🔟 Nightspots

The bar at Abraxas

1 Abraxas, Palma
One of Palma's top clubs and located along the waterfront, this huge place specializes in loud house music. As with nightlife venues all over Spain, the action doesn't get going until about 1am – so don't arrive early and be considered hopelessly naïve or desperate! It's a mixed crowd at all times, though there are regular gay-themed nights in season. ◈ Avda. Gabriel Roca, 42 • 971 455908 • www.abraxasmallorca.com • Adm

2 Tito's, Palma
Palma's other huge nightlife venue is popular with a younger crowd, from teens to 20-somethings. The décor is all very modern, with lots of stainless steel in evidence, and the light show and sound system are, of course, up-to-the-minute, the music ranging from house to top-40. Sunday night is Gay Night. ◈ Entrances from Paseo Maritimo and Plaça Gomila, 3 • 971 730017 • www.titosmallorca.com

3 Sa Posada de Bellver, Palma
Located just above Plaça Gomila, this idiosyncratic, friendly little place will remind you of a gypsy encampment. Expect live ethnic music most nights, and an eclectic range of non-Spanish foods – Middle Eastern finger foods and other exotic treats. It isn't remote, but it feels that way. ◈ C/Bellver, 7 • 971 730739

4 Gran Casino Mallorca, Urbanización Sol de Mallorca, Magaluf
This Las Vegas-style casino and nightclub is more than just a glitzy gambling destination, there is an excellent restaurant and in summer they offer a programme of concerts from classical to jazz. Smart dress (see p101).

Gran Casino Mallorca

For more top nightspots on the Southwest Coast **see p101**, on the North Coast **p109**, and on the Southeast Coast **p119**

Chivas

5 Barracuda, Port d'Andratx

Keep an eye out for this club's posters all around the port – they're particularly original and collectible, the work of Jorge Bascones. The vivacious young woman who runs the spacious place is very talented at dreaming up new theme nights that manage to appeal to just about everyone in town – at least to all those who enjoy bopping the night away *(see p101)*.

6 BCM Planet Dance, Magaluf

The biggest dance club on the island regularly hosts such star DJs as Judge Jules and Tim Westwood. The cavernous internal space is put to good use with some incredible laser shows, and there are also 16 canons, which fire anything from foam to confetti into the lively crowds. ✪ *Avda. S'Olivera • 971 711856 • Adm*

7 Chivas, Port de Pollença

After you've revved up at Port de Pollença's pubs, then strolled around the promenades and central square to check out the endless stream of attractive young people, this is the place to make for next. Nothing unusual about it, but it's the disco of choice for the 20-something cognoscenti – at least for the moment – who come here to dance till dawn, go back to the hotel for 40 winks, then hit the beach *(see p109)*.

8 Menta, Port d'Alcúdia

This is a well-run club with an exciting range of rooms and areas for full-on partying, having a quiet drink with friends, or even taking a nighttime dip in a pool fit for an emperor. It's a beautiful and inviting place, run with an unerring sense of style and good taste – it's glitzy, of course, but never tacky. The location is a bit off the beaten track, but it's worth whatever it takes to get there *(see p109)*.

9 Es Carreró, Portocristo

This little street, quiet and unassuming by day, turns into the hub of the resort at night. Innumerable tiny music-drinks-dance venues open up, and the young, beautiful, and restless turn out in droves to partake of the varied pleasures – all of them decked out in their best mylar and polyester finery. It's a stirring sight, and the air positively vibrates with all the pumping beats that emanate from every doorway *(see p119)*.

10 Opio Bar, Palma

Popular with Palma's jet set visitors, the Opio Bar is in the Hotel Puro, one of a few boutique hotels that have made the Mallorcan capital chic again. The decor is minimalist white with dashes of red and the sounds played by the resident DJ are laid-back cool. ✪ *Hotel Puro, C/Monte Negro, 12 • 971 425450 • 8pm–2am*

Opio Bar, Palma

Following pages **Cala Formentor**

Left **Dylan sign** Centre **Aries Hotel** Right **Black Cat sign**

Gay and Lesbian Venues in Palma

Ben Amics Association
This group provides Mallorca with its pink hotline – only two hours a day, weekdays, but it's a great connection for new arrivals.There are get-togethers from time to time, including a sort of café that opens sporadically. ◈ *C/Conqustador, 2* • *900 777500* • *9pm Mon–Fri* • *Not available in Aug*

Café Lorca
Just off Plaça Gomila, and down a few steps, this friendly hangout is where locals congregate, so it's a good chance to find out what the scene is really like from those who live it. ◈ *C/Garcia Lorca, 21* • *10am–late*

Aries Hotel, Club & Sauna
A large, comfortable hotel, with its own nightclub and exclusively gay sauna, located on the street that's action-central for gay life on the island. The friendly staff are Scandinavian, Dutch, English, German and other nationalities, and they all do their best to create a fun atmosphere. ◈ *C/Porres, 3* • *971 737899* • *www.ariesmallorca.com*

Marcos
The subdued lighting in violet tones and the classical statuary dotted around may seem a bit passé, but there's always a good turnout, usually of 30- and 40-somethings. It's a quiet alternative to the mostly frenetic life in the other bars and clubs. ◈ *Avda. Joan Miró, 54* • *971 286144* • *From 10pm*

Dylan
A lively choice – probably because of the gay videos that are always playing. The place is open to the street at one end, so there always seems to be something happening or about to happen. ◈ *Avda. Joan Miró, 68* • *10pm–3am*

Rosamar Hotel & Bar
This rainbow hotel is the place to stay if you want to be where all the action is. Its patio bar is where the international mix of young and beautiful A-list gays congregates before heading off to the dance floor. ◈ *Avda. Joan Miró, 74* • *971 732723* • *From 11pm* • *Mar–Dec* • *www.rosamarpalma.com*

Café Lorca

Almost all of Palma's gay and lesbian venues are lined up in an area called La Gomila, west of the city centre

Rosamar Hotel

Bar Status
A long-standing favourite, Bar Status is a relaxed, welcoming bar catering to a slightly older crowd. It is a good place to start the night, and the friendly staff will happily give tips on where to go. Ⓢ *Avda. Joan Miró, 38 • 10pm–3am*

N.P.I. Pub
This is mainly one for the girls, although it does attract a mixed crowd. Low, mellow music and a chilled-out atmosphere make it the perfect spot to get together with friends. Ⓢ *C/Industria, 27 • 10pm–3am*

Black Cat
The cover charge here will get you in not only to dance and check everybody out, but also to be regaled with a stage show that generally features both drag acts and male "exotic dancers". Ⓢ *Avda. Joan Miró, 75 • From midnight*

Bruixeries
The name of this tiny, lesbian-run disco/bar means "spells", and every few months a white witch comes in to give it the once-over. Downstairs there is a resident DJ and upstairs you will find a pool table. The crowd is young and pretty but exclusively female. Ⓢ *C/Estanc, 9 • 9pm–3am.*

Top 10 Gay/Lesbian Areas Outside Palma

1 Platja y Dique del Oeste
Located at Porto Pi, near downtown Palma, this is a noted gay-friendly beach.

2 Platja El Mago
Near Portals Vells and Magalluf, on the western end of Palma Bay, this is a recognized nudist beach.

3 Cala Blava
The "Blue Cove" is a popular gay section of the vast beach area along S'Arenal, on the eastern curve of Palma Bay.

4 El Bosque
At the northern end of S'Arenal, "The Woods" also attracts gay revellers.

5 Es Carnatge
Closest to Palma on the eastern side, at Ca'n Pastilla, this is another popular gay gathering point.

6 Valle de la Luna
An association offering a cultural and artistic exchange platform for mainly German and Spanish women in the Sóller area. Ⓢ *971 634889 • www.vallemallorca.de*

7 Platja de Muro
Just to the north of C'an Picafort and south of Port d'Alcúdia, this beach is a congregation point for gays.

8 Cala es Gulló
One of several handsome coves just to the north of Cala Rajada, this one is particularly known for being gay-friendly.

9 Punta de N'Amer
South of hyper-busy Cala Millor, the excellent beach here is full of international gay vibes.

10 Platja Es Trenc
The island's finest unspoiled beach, a place for nudists and alternative sun-worshippers of all sorts (see p43).

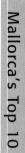

Left **Carved ham** Centre **Olives** Right **An ensaïmada**

Culinary Highlights

1 Pa amb Oli

This is the favourite Mallorcan (and greater Catalonian) snack – a regional version of the more internationally known bruschetta. The basic item is sliced baguette rubbed with garlic then smeared with fresh tomato, drizzled with olive oil and sprinkled with salt. To this basic recipe, you can add whatever you please – usually ham and/or cheese. The vibrant flavour is utterly irresistible.

Seafood paella

2 Frit Mallorquí and Llom amb Col

Frit is cheap peasant food at its heaviest, consisting of fried offal of the famous black Mallorcan pig, cooked in oil with potatoes and onions. You'll find it at its savoury best in some of the more traditional market towns of Es Pla. *Llom amb col*, pork wrapped in cabbage, is equally traditional and substantial.

3 Tumbet

The vegetables that go to make up this stew can vary widely, depending on the season, but classically comprise a selection from among the following: aubergine (eggplant), bell peppers, courgettes (zucchini), onions, cabbage and potatoes. Seasoning consists mainly of garlic.

4 Sopes Mallorquinas

By far the best of Mallorca's *sopes* (soups) is fish soup, a hearty stew of shellfish and white fish in a broth flavoured with garlic and saffron. It may also contain rice or pasta for added body. Other soups common on the island are concoctions of vegetables and mixed meats, often seasoned with garlic.

5 Arròs

Arròs (rice) dishes include: the familiar *paella Valenciana*, saffron rice with a mixture of seafood, fish, chicken and sausage; *arròs brut*, rice with offal; and *arròs negre*, rice with seafood cooked using squid ink.

6 Pork Sausages

Mallorca's most prized sausage, *sobrassada*, comes from the island's famous small black

Cheeses and sausages, Pollença market

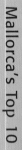

Baked fish in rock salt

pigs. It's tender, flavourful and tinged red from spices, and you'll find various versions of it, including a *sobrassada* pâté for spreading on toast.

Sea Bass Baked in Rock Salt

The Mallorcan version of this classic is the *pièce de résistance* wherever it is served. The salt pack keeps the moisture and flavour safely inside, and when it is cracked open you find the most delicate, succulent fish, with just a hint of saltiness to add piquancy.

Ensaïmades

These unbelievably light and flaky spiral pastries are the pride of the island. They can be dusted with icing sugar or filled with candied fruits or jam.

Vi de la Casa

Mallorca is now enjoying a decided upswing in its wine production, and you can generally depend on the house wines to be very good. The reds are considered the island's best at the moment, being robust and aromatic, though some whites attain a lively fruitiness.

Canya

Canya is the term to use in a bar when you want them to pull you a draught beer; for a large one ask for a *jerra*. *Cervesa* (beer) tends to be of the pilsner type, though in Palma you can find a local variety that is black, fizzy and bitter.

Top 10 Tapas Types

1 Pickled and Cured
The easiest finger-nibbles: olives (sometimes very salty), miniature pickles and possibly pearl onions. A cured favourite is salted cod.

2 Marinated
All manner of seafood, including anchovies, sardines and shellfish, steeped in pale green olive oil.

3 Smoked
You'll find sliced smoked ham everywhere, along with the local sausage, *sobrassada*.

4 With Mayonnaise
A big favourite is *patatas bravas*, fried potato cubes with mayonnaise and spicy red sauce. Another is aïoli, a pungent, but delicious, mix of garlic and mayonnaise.

5 On Bread
The signature bread snack is a crust of baguette with olive oil and maybe other toppings (*see pa amb oli opposite*).

6 Egg-Based
Truita espanyol is a potato, egg and onion pie, served by the slice. Omelettes, possibly with prawns, are also common.

7 Fried
Calamari rings are most popular, but you'll also see fish and chicken croquettes.

8 Grilled or Roasted
From snails roasted with garlic to grilled baby squid, octopus, aubergine, kebabs and sweet bell peppers.

9 Stewed or Steamed
As well as *tumbet* (*see opposite*), steamed shellfish, broad green beans and artichokes shouldn't be missed.

10 Pâté
Another signature island dish is pork liver pâté.

For drinking and eating tips see p137

79

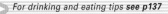

Left **The ubiquitous morning cup of coffee** Centre **Gran Café 1919** Right **Mestizo sign**

🔟 Cafés and Bars

Abaco

1 Abaco, Palma

Many can hardly believe their eyes when they first find this gorgeous place, set in the courtyard of a period townhouse. Candlelit, full of fresh flowers and fruit, and with the delightful touch of tropical birds in the magical garden, it is surely the best place in the world to have a drink *(see p92)*. Outside of town, the same people run Abacanto, where they've done a similar thing to an entire mansion.

2 Grand Café Cappuccino, Palma

An elegant 18th-century palace set around a palm-filled patio houses this charming café. The dining areas have been smartly refurbished but do not have the appeal of the romantic courtyard

Grand Café Cappuccino

with its pretty stone fountain. Drinks, snacks and full meals are served here. There are three branches of the Grand Café Cappuccino in Palma and one in Calvià to the west of Palma. ⊛ *Palma: C/Sant Miguel, 53; 971 719764 • Paseo de Mar, 18; 971 681368 • Paseo Marítmo, 1 (Avda. Gabriel Roca); 971 282162 • Calvia: Puerto Portals, 18; 971 677293*

3 Garito Café, Palma

A long-established arty café, the Garito was revamped a few years ago to become one of Palma's top night spots. Stylish retro decor, excellent music and a breezy terrace. It is mellow by day but heats up at night. ⊛ *Darsena de Can Barbera s/n • 971 736912 • www. garitocafe.com*

4 Es Grau, Carretera Andratx-Estellencs

This roadside café is located right next to the Mirador Ricardo Roca *(see p48)*, and shares the same great views of the entire coast. You can get drinks, snacks or a complete fill-up here before you hit the road again. Don't miss browsing through the unusual gift shop on the site – amid all the tourist junk that has little to do with Mallorca, you'll find some pretty pottery.

Es Grau roadside café by the Mirador Ricardo Roca viewpoint

cream and soaking up the laid-back atmosphere of the town. It's also an ideal listening post for the musical entertainment at the nearby park *(see p117)*.

5 Agapanto, Port de Sóller

This elegant bar-restaurant, on the harbour at Playa d'en Repic, has deckchairs on the sand and a flower-filled terrace. Try one of their delicious Cava cocktails. There's occasional live music, wine tastings and other events. ◈ *Ca. del Faro, 2 • 971 633860 • www.agapanto.com*

6 Gran Café 1919, Port de Pollença

An ideal corner location on an elegant promenade has been claimed by this old-fashioned café (similar to one in Port d'Alcúdia, *see p107*). The staff are done up in black ties, and the décor evokes Belle Époque style with a frothy dash of Catalan Modernista. ◈ *Anglada Camarassa & Passeig Voramar • Map E1*

7 Mestizo Café, Port d'Alcúdia

Resembling something from the American Southwest, with warm adobe colours and desert decor, this place is a block off the beach and popular for cocktails, coffee and cakes. Internet access is also available. Open evenings only. ◈ *C/Coral • Map F2*

8 Sa Pedra, Porto Cristo

Head here if you want to gaze out on Porto Cristo's inlet and picturesque palisades while lingering over a drink or fancy ice

9 Café Sa Plaça, Santanyí

The whole town of Santanyí is architecturally interesting, especially the central square, and this is the ideal spot from which to take it in. The town is surprisingly sophisticated, due to the huge influx of international residents, the majority of whom have brought a lot of money with them. Still, local customs and atmosphere have not been lost, and this café offers a nice mix of contemporary pizzazz and rural relaxation *(see p117)*.

10 Café Sa Plaça, Sineu

At this café-restaurant in the town's central square, you can take in a view of the magnificent church of Santa María as you enjoy your meal. On Wednesdays you can also watch the spectacle of the vibrant local market. This café is the place to sample a time-honoured *orxata*, a sweet, creamy soft drink made from tiger nuts *(see p124)*.

Café Sa Plaça

For more popular cafés and bars in Palma see p92, and pp99, 101, 107, 109, 117, 119 & 124 for the rest of Mallorca

Left **Traffic** Centre **Miramar** Right **Read's Hotel**

🔟 Restaurants

Refectori, Palma

pergola combine to make it one of the island's most beautiful spots. As well as an International-Mediterranean fusion menu, they serve excellent paella. ◈ *Carretera de Deià, km 56.1 • Map C2 • 971 638280 • www.casxorc.com • No dis acc • €€€€€*

1 Refectori, Palma

Water, stone and steel have been used to create a minimalist interior in this stylish restaurant. The cuisine uses local ingredients, such as Sóller shrimps, Mallorcan oil and Máo cheese, but with a daring twist. Expect dishes like veal in coffee sauce and fresh fish with olives and broth. Booking recommended. ◈ *C/de la Missió 7a, Palma • Map N2 • 971 227347 • €€€*

2 Vent de Tramuntana, Port d'Andratx

On a patio with palm, olive and oleander trees and enclosed by an old stone wall, this is rural gourmet dining at its peak. Dishes might include roasted duck with mango sauce, braised potato slices and perfectly al dente green beans. ◈ *C/Can Perot, 9 • Map A4 • 971 671756 • Closed Tue • €€€*

3 Ca's Xorc, Sóller

This exquisite mountain eyrie was supermodel Claudia Schiffer's choice for celebrating her 30th birthday. The lush gardens, tropical birds, fountains, exotic Moroccan touches and bougainvillea-covered

4 Bens d'Avall, Deià-Sóller

The spectacular terrace affords one of the island's greatest views. Fresh fish is cooked in a wood-burning oven, and every ingredient is carefully selected from the best and the freshest Mallorca has to offer. The fresh pasta of herbs and summer mushrooms with a light Mahon cheese and basil sauce is typically good *(see p100)*.

5 Ca N'Antuna, Fornalutx

Featuring a very small menu of typical Mallorcan cuisine, with offerings changing depending on the season's best, this unpretentious place is set in a precipitous valley with magnificent mountain views. Offerings might include a

Bens d'Avall

This is a summary of the best restaurants across the island. For many more regional listings see pp93, 100, 108, 118 & 125

L'Hermitage

Mallorcan garden soup, battered calamari, rabbit, suckling pig and various omelettes. ◈ C/Arbona Colom 8 • Map D2 • 971 633068 • Closed Sun D, Mon • €€

Traffic, Alaró

Dine on the main town square, in elegant dining rooms or in a lush back garden featuring one of the few private lawns on the island. All is peace and tranquillity, and the cuisine is tempting variations of time-honoured recipes. Fresh fish, often served with a sauce of prawns and mussels, is a forte. ◈ Plaça de la Vila, 8 • Map D3 • 971 879 117 • Closed Tue • www.canxim.com • Limited dis acc • €€€

L'Hermitage, Orient

Very off the beaten track, but worth the trip for the soaring views and some of Mallorca's best cuisine. The setting, in elegant medieval rooms and terraces nestled amid luxuriant copses, is also unforgettable. Prepared by a top Swedish chef, dishes such as loin of lamb with dried apricots and a crispy vegetable roll are a must. ◈ Hotel l'Hermitage, Ctra. Alaró-Bunyola • Map D3 • 971 180303 • www.hermitage-hotel.com • Closed Nov–Dec • €€€€€

La Fonda, Pollença

The wood-beamed medieval interior features a nice mix of contemporary art and rustic antiques, or you can sit outside on a breezy side street. Roast kid is a speciality as well as, in spring, calçots (large leek-like vegetables) with salsa Romesco (red peppers, vinegar, oil, almonds and walnuts). ◈ C/Antoni Maura 32 • Map E1 • 971 534751 • Closed Mon • €€€

Miramar, Port d'Alcúdia

Not far from the seafront and centrally located on the promenade, this excellent choice is almost always busy but the high-quality professional service never suffers. Seafood and fish are the highlights; the fish soup with rice and lobster or the fried lobster with crispy bread are mouthwatering winners. ◈ Passeig Marítim, 2 • Map F2 • 971 545293 • €€€€

Bacchus (Read's Hotel), Santa Maria del Camí

Arguably, this establishment serves the most perfect food on the island, brought to you by superbly trained waiting staff in an exquisite dining room or on a terrace under the stars. Its Michelin star is well-deserved, and chef Marc Fosh is a true master of creative excellence – every bite is pure pleasure (see p125).

Bacchus interior

AROUND
THE ISLAND

MALLORCA'S TOP 10

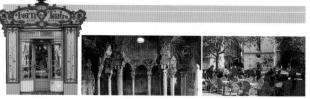

Left **Forn des Teatre shop** Centre **Banys Àrabs** Right **Cafés outside Santa Eulalia**

Palma

I N 1983, PALMA BECAME *the capital of the newly created Autonomous Community of the Balearic Islands and transformed itself from a provincial town into a metropolis. Today, it has over 300,000 inhabitants and captivates all visitors as it once captivated Jaume I, who, after conquering it in 1229 described it as the "loveliest town that I have ever seen". It is pleasant to stroll along the clean, attractive streets past renovated historic buildings. The town and harbour are full of life, with bars and restaurants busy with locals and tourists alike.*

Flower stall, La Rambla

🔟 Sights in Palma

1. Cathedral
2. Palau de l'Almudaina
3. Museu Diocesà
4. Banys Àrabs
5. Museu de Mallorca
6. Basílica de Sant Francesc
7. Plaça Weyler
8. Ca'n Solleric and Passeig des Born
9. Castell de Bellver
10. Fundació Pilar i Joan Miró

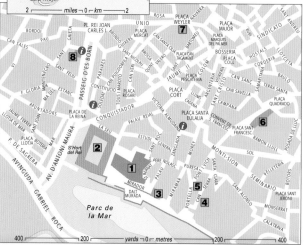

Previous pages **Deià**

Mudéjar (Spanish-Moorish) style; and the jasper sarcophagus of Jaume II, which stood in the cathedral until 1904. The palace itself, which is built around a large courtyard, adjoins the city walls *(see also p62).*
🔊 *C/Mirador, 5 • Map M5 • 10am–2pm Mon–Sat • Adm*

Mallorca Cathedral

1 Cathedral
Dominating the entire port, Mallorca Cathedral (known as La Seu) is a glowing man-made mountain of sandstone. The second largest Gothic cathedral in the world, it is also the symbol of the city and the island's most visited building *(see pp8–9).*
🔊 *Map L5–M5*

2 Palau de l'Almudaina
Having been a royal palace for over 1,000 years, this building's style speaks of its long, fractious history with an uneasy blending of Islamic and Gothic elements *(see pp10–11).* 🔊 *Map L4*

3 Museu Diocesà
Situated just behind the cathedral, the 17th-century Palau Episcopal houses a little diocese museum. On display are some fascinating items from various churches around Mallorca, as well as a selection of majolica tiles. Particularly noteworthy are: a picture of St George slaying the dragon in front of Palma's city gate, painted in 1468–70 by Pere Nisart; Bishop Galiana's panel depicting the life of St Paul (who is portrayed holding a sword); the Gothic pulpit in a

4 Banys Àrabs
This 10th-century brick *hammam* (bath house) is one of the few architectural reminders of a Moorish presence on Mallorca. A small horseshoe-arched chamber, with a dome supported by irregular columns and what would once have been under-floor heating, has survived in its original form. This would have been the *tepidarium*, the luke-warm room; there would have also been a hot room and a cold plunge. Apart from this, there's not much to see, but the pleasant garden has tables and chairs.
🔊 *C/Can Serra, 7 • Map M–N5 • 9am–7:30pm daily (Dec–Mar to 6pm) • Adm*

Palau de l'Almudaina

Museu de Mallorca

It's worth the entrance fee just to see the building, a 17th-century palace built on the foundations of one of Mallorca's earliest Arab houses. The museum contains some fascinating exhibits, providing a quick overview of Mallorca from prehistory to the 20th century. There are some powerful recreations of Neolithic and Bronze Age tombs and dwellings, and several treasures from Roman times. Some gorgeous examples of Modernista furniture are on the top floor – in particular a console with a daringly asymmetrical design *(see also p62)*. ◈ *C/de la Portella, 5 • Map M5 • 971 717540 • 10am–2pm & 5–7pm Tue–Sat (6–9pm Thu), 10am–2pm Sun • Adm*

Statue, Museu de Mallorca

Basilica de Sant Francesc

During the Middle Ages, this was Palma's most fashionable church, and to be buried here was a major status symbol. Aristrocratic families competed with each other by building ever more ostentatious sarcophagi in which to place their dead. The dark interior contains many fine works of art. Next to a 17th-century statue of the Madonna is the carved figure of the famous medieval mystic Ramon Llull,

who is buried in the church. Standing in front of the basilica is a statue of Junipero Serra, a Franciscan monk and native of Mallorca, who was sent to California in 1768 and founded Los Angeles and San Francisco *(see also p58)*. ◈ *Plaça Sant Francesc • Map N4 • 971 712695 • 9:30am–12:30pm & 3:30–6pm daily, closed Sun afternoon • Adm*

Plaça Weyler

Several interesting examples of Palma's Modernista output are found in this square. The Gran Hotel was Palma's first luxury hotel when it opened in 1903. Designed by Catalan architect Lluis Domenech i Muntaner, it was the building that began the craze for Modernista in the city and is now an excellent free art gallery, CaixaForum, with a

The Highest-End Tourism

Although cheap package tourism dominates much of Palma, plenty of upper-crust visitors make Palma Bay their summer destination. The choicest spot is Port Portals, where King Juan Carlos I and Queen Sofía often berth at the swishest yacht club of them all. Be aware that prices reflect the world-class jetsetter status of the well-heeled habitués.

Left **Plaça Weyler** Right **Grounds of the Fundació Pilar i Joan Miró**

Castell de Bellver

permanent display of paintings by Hermen Anglada-Camarasa and a major venue for temporary exhibitions. Across the street is the wonderful façade of the Forn des Teatre pastry shop next to the old-fashioned Bar Central (see p92). ◈ Map M3

8 Casa Solleric and Passeig des Born

A fine Italianate edifice, Casa Solleric was built for a family of olive oil merchants in 1763 and converted into a modern art gallery in 1995. It stands at the top of the gracious Passeig des Born, which was created in the 19th century on a dried-up riverbed. This is Palma's main promenade, similar to Barcelona's famous Ramblas and the venue of large-scale cultural events. Set among its plane trees are flowerbeds and seats. ◈ Map K–L3 • Casa Solleric 10am–2pm & 5–9pm Tue–Sat, 10am–1:30pm Sun • Free

9 Castell de Bellver

One of Europe's most remarkable, fairytale castles was actually a prison for 700 years and now houses an excellent museum (see pp12–13). ◈ Map R1

10 Fundació Pilar i Joan Miró

The prolific career of Catalan master Joan Miró in all its depth and variety: few artists have had such a brilliant showcase built for them (see pp14–15). ◈ Map R2

A Walk Around Old Palma

Mid-Morning

🕐 This circular walk takes two to four hours and starts in Plaça Joan Carles I, just at the top of the **Passeig des Born**. From here, walk east on La Unió to **Plaça Weyler**, where you can buy pastries at the Forn des Teatre and see the exhibitions in the Gran Hotel.

Climb the steps to the right of the Teatre Principal until you get to Plaça Major. In this beautiful arcaded square, you'll see street artists and performers, and you can stop for a drink in one of the cafés.

Come out of the Plaça along Carrer Sant Miquel. Stop at the **Museu Fundación Juan March** (see p90) and the charming Església de Sant Miquel.

Now double back through Plaça Major to view the façades of **L'Aquila** and **Can Rei** (p90). Go down Carrer Argenteria to visit the **Església de Santa Eulàlia** (p90), and then Carrer Morey to take in **Ca N'Oleza** (p90).

Late Morning

Continue on Carrer Miramar, past glorious **Palacio Ca Sa Galesa** hotel (p140), to exit at the broad seawall, where you can look up at the **Cathedral** (pp8–9).

Visit the cathedral and **Palau de l'Almudaina** (pp10–11), then go down to the **S'Hort del Rei** gardens (p64). Finally, stroll up the Born and have a snack at **Bar Bosch** (p92) on the square where you started, or head to a restaurant for a more substantial lunch (p93).

Left **City walls, Parc de la Mar** Centre **Figure at Santa Eulalia** Right **Ancient olive tree, Plaça Cort**

Best of the Rest

1 Parc de la Mar
The park next to the cathedral is a popular spot, with a lake, cafés and open-air concerts *(see also p48 & 64)*. ✆ *Map K–P5*

2 Ca N'Oleza
This aristocratic mansion has one of the most elegant of the famous Palma patios, with fabulous wrought-iron railings, a Gothic stairway and graceful balustrades. ✆ *C/Morey, 9 • Map M5*

3 Templar Gate
A fortified gate marks the former entrance to the 13th-century headquarters of the Knights Templar, built when the wealthy brotherhood was in full power. The buildings are now privately owned. ✆ *C/Temple • Map P5*

4 Can Vivot
Peep in on another of Palma's grand courtyards, with Corinthian columns and balustraded balcony. Its sumptuous library, filled with scientific instruments from the Enlightenment era, is sometimes open. ✆ *C/Can Savellà, 2 • Map N4*

5 Església de Santa Eulalia
Built in the mid-1200s in Gothic style, the church was completely remodelled in the 19th century and contains one of the most bombastic altarpieces of them all *(see also p58)*. ✆ *Map N4*

6 Plaça Cort
With its elegant façades, including the town hall, and ancient olive tree, this is one of Palma's loveliest squares. ✆ *Map M4*

7 L'Aquila/Can Rei
Two striking examples of Palma's Modernista architecture. L'Aquila combines Catalan Modernista elements with Viennese tendencies, while Can Rei owes much to Antonio Gaudí. ✆ *Map N3*

8 Museu Fundación Juan March
Includes works by Picasso, Dalí, Miró and Juan Gris. ✆ *C/Sant Miguel, 11 • Map M2 • 10am–6:30pm Mon–Fri, 10:30am–2pm Sat*

9 Sa Llotja
This handsome, 15th-century seafront building was the city's Exchange and is now a cultural centre. ✆ *Passeig Sagrera • Map K4 • 971 711705 • Open during exhibitions*

10 Es Baluard, Museu d'Art Modern i Contemporani
Includes art and sculptures by Cézanne, Gauguin and Picasso. ✆ *Plaça Porta de Santa Catalina 10 • Map J3 • 971 908200 • 10am–8pm Tue–Sun (to 9pm mid-Jun–Sep) • Adm*

For more on Palma's gardens see pp64–5

Left **Zara** Centre **Loewe** Right **Imaginarium**

TOP 10 Shops

1 Zara
Hip, affordable clothing for the entire family. Service is a bit hit or miss, but you'll find the linen blends and light cottons just right for the island climate. Has scents and sunglasses, too. ⦿ *Es Born, 25*

2 Persepolis
Palma's premier antiques shop has major works of religious sculpture, Old Master paintings, important period furniture, oriental carpets and small silver and enamel pieces. ⦿ *Avda. Jaume III, 23*

3 Loewe
Upmarket fashions from Madrid: handbags, sunglasses, perfumes, vibrant scarves, leather and linen, silky suede, travel bags, and shoes, all in a setting that's elegant without being snooty. ⦿ *Avda. Jaume III, 1, Corner Jaume III & Born*

4 Imaginarium
Games, dolls, construction toys, books, furniture and beach things for children under eight. ⦿ *Pl. Mercat, 8*

5 Flor de Fil
A historic shop selling artisan, traditional Mallorcan embroidery, including the typical Mallorcan cross stitch, point stitch and chain stitch. The perfect place to find a refined gift or souvenir unique to the island. ⦿ *C/Apuntadors, 3*

6 Colmado Santo Domingo
Every foodstuff made on the island is here, including cheeses, *sobrassada*, fig loaves, brandies, wines, fruits, nuts, sauces and pickles. An impressive array of cured meats are strung from the ceiling. ⦿ *C/S. Santo Domingo, 1*

7 Relojería Alemana
Designer watches, fine jewellery, silver tableware and Mallorcan grandfather clocks. ⦿ *C/Colom, 14; also Jaume III, 26*

8 Fiol Llibres
Secondhand books in various languages, run by a lady who knows her stock. ⦿ *C/Oms, 45-A*

9 Fet a Mà
Palma has many handicraft shops: this is about the best, with well-chosen pottery, glass and more from across Spain in traditional and contemporary designs. ⦿ *C/Sant Miquel, 52*

10 Horrach Moyá
A commercial gallery showcasing contemporary, avant-garde Mallorcan artists. ⦿ *C/Catalunya, 4*

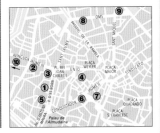

For the best general shopping areas in Palma **see p70**

Left **Café des Casal Solleric** Centre **Café Lírico** Right **Bar Central**

Cafés and Bars

1 El Pesquero
Located directly on the water. Have tapas with your drink, or be tempted by the set menu of the day. ○ C/ Moll de la Llotja • 971 715220

2 Abaco
Perhaps the world's most romantic setting for drinks: an ancient courtyard and lush garden, with hundreds of fresh fruits, huge bouquets of fresh flowers, exotic birds twittering, soft candle-light and perfumed air (see also p80). ○ C/ Sant Joan, 1 • 971 714939

3 Café Lírico
Retro bar with photos of old Palma, mirrors, marble and Mod-ernista touches. Fresh juices include maracuya (passion fruit), mango, red papaya and guava. ○ Avda. Antonio Maura, 6 • 971 721125

4 Café des Casal Solleric
Housed in a historic building, ideal for people-watching, this welcoming café plays hip music and has a local feel. ○ Es Born, 27 • 971 728428

5 Bar Bosch
Perpetually busy and the most central bar of all, it's great for tapas and a drink any time of day. ○ Plaça Rei Joan Carles I

6 Blue Jazz Bar, Palma
This cool, roof-top bar hosts live jazz on Thursday, Friday and Saturday nights. ○ Hotel Saratoga, Paseo Mallorca 6 • 971 727240

7 Azul Cyber Café, Palma
Mallorca's oldest cyber café has efficient equipment, fast connections and personal laptop facilities. It is cheap and friendly, with expert staff from the adjacent Azul computer shop. ○ C/Soledad 2 • 971 712927

8 Bar Central
Tapas, bocadillos (sandwiches) and pastries in a classic, slightly fly-blown place. ○ Plaça Weyler, 10 • 971 721058

9 Ca'n Joan de S'aigo
Since 1700, this popular rococo delight has been serving chocolate, orjata (almond milk), ice cream and pastries. Expect to wait a bit. ○ C/C'an Sanç, 10; C/Baró de Santa Maria del Sepulcre, 5

10 Forn des Teatre
A 19th-century bakery specializing in ensaïmadas, (typical Mallorcan pastries), and other local delicacies. The adjacent café, with its outdoor tables, is the perfect place for breakfast or a snack. Open until 1am. ○ Plaza Weyler, 9 • 971 727383

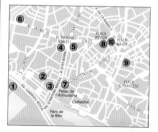

For Palma's top nightclubs see p72; for gay and lesbian venues see pp76–7

Price Categories

For a three-course meal for one with half a bottle of wine (or equivalent meal), taxes and extra charges.

€	under €20
€€	€20–€30
€€€	€30–€40
€€€€	€40–€50
€€€€€	over €50

Left **Asador Tierra Aranda** Right **Celler Sa Premsa**

🔟 Places to Eat

1 Caballito del Mar

One of Palma's top places. Delicious cuisine, from mango soup to marinated salmon carpaccio. 🕸 *Passeig Sagrera, 5 • 971 721074 • daily (Oct–May: Tue–Sun) • €€€€€*

2 La Bóveda

Charming restaurant in the old fish market. Food is mainly Basque-Castilian, including tapas; wine is drunk directly from a wineskin. 🕸 *C/Boteria, 3 • 971 714863 • Mar–Jan: Mon–Sat • €€€€*

3 Aramis

The focus is creative and original Mediterranean cuisine, with a weekly tasting menu for dedicated foodies. 🕸 *C/Montenegro, 1 • 971 725232 • Tue–Fri, Sat D • €€€€*

4 Bon Lloc

A fusion of the Mediterranean and Asia at Palma's best vegetarian restaurant. 🕸 *C/Sant Feliu, 7 • 971 718617 • Mon–Sat (lunch only) • Limited dis acc • €*

5 Rossini

The owner is from Puglia in Italy, so the *mozzarella di bufala* is juicy and tangy, and the pasta is nicely al dente. 🕸 *C/Pi, 4 • 971 720235 • Mon–Sat • €€€€*

6 El Pilón

Friendly place with hip music. An extensive menu includes artichokes, oysters and *tumbet* (vegetable stew). 🕸 *Restaurante Marisquería, C/Gifre, 4 • 971 726034 • Mon–Sat • No dis acc • Parking • €€€*

7 Asador Tierra Aranda

Service is carried out with panache in a stone-paved garden with marquees, in which you'll enjoy a dinner of Castilian cooking. Lunch is served indoors, in stately rooms. 🕸 *C/Concepción, 4 • 971 714256 • Tue–Sat, Sun lunch • No dis acc • €€€*

8 C'an Carlos

Mallorcan cooking at its very best, with wonderful bread and olives, seafood, fish, lamb, pâté and delicious house wines. 🕸 *C/ de S'Aigua 5 • 971 713869 • Mon lunch, Tue–Sat • No dis acc • €€€€*

9 Celler Sa Premsa

Set your sights on classics like cabbage rolls with pork, and paella. 🕸 *Plaça Bisbe Berenguer de Palou, 8 • 971 723529 • Mon–Sat (Mon–Fri in Jul & Aug) • Limited dis acc • €€*

10 Aquiara

Tapas and main courses with a difference: inventive chef Koldo Roy creates delights such as veal-tail hamburger and potatoes stuffed with foie gras. 🕸 *Passeig Maritim, 3 • 971 732435 • Mon–Sat • No dis acc • €€€*

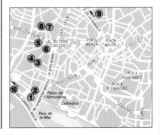

Note: *Unless otherwise stated, all restaurants have disabled access, accept credit cards and include vegetarian dishes*

Left **Café, Es Port** Centre **Sa Granja** Right **Gazebo, Son Marroig**

Southwest Coast

I F, AS SOME SAY, *the island's shape suggests a billy-goat facing west, the southwestern coastline makes up his long face while he sniffs the flower petal of Illa Dragonera. In winter, the mountains of this region act as a buffer, shielding the central*

Image of Santa Catalina, Valldemossa

plain from the fierce tramuntana wind and absorbing most of the island's rain and snow; in summer, they provide a cool retreat, mostly for well-heeled residents and visitors, from the heat of Palma and the south.

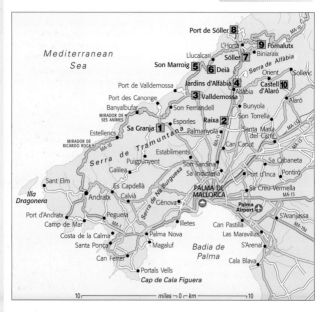

Share your travel recommendations on traveldk.com

Valldemossa

1 La Granja

Experience a complete cross-section of traditional Mallorcan life at this fully restored, noble country estate *(see pp16–17)*. ◈ Map B3

2 Raixa

In the 18th century, Mallorcan country homes became a symbol of prestige, and this one, built by Cardinal Antonio Despuig, is one of the finest examples. The Cardinal was an antiquarian and so adorned his Italianate estate with Classical statuary to complement the grand Neoclassical staircase. The parterres are laid out in the Italian taste of the day, with Classical touches such as fountains and a belvedere, and picturesque medieval references. ◈ Map C3 • Palma-Soller road, km 12.2, Bunyola • 10am–2pm Sat & Sun; guided visits by appt Mon–Fri • Adm

3 Valldemossa

It was in Valldemossa, Mallorca's highest and one of its prettiest towns, that lovers Frédéric Chopin and George Sand spent one dramatic winter in the early 19th century. The result was Sand's infamous book *A Winter in Majorca*, both a scathing indictment of the island's people and their ways and a poetic rhapsody in praise of the natural beauties of the place *(see pp18–21 & also p63 for the museum)*. ◈ Map C3

4 Jardins d'Alfàbia

This oasis of heavenly peace high in the mountains was designed by Arab landscape architects 1,000 years ago as an image of Paradise. The gardens have been reworked over the centuries, mostly with Gothic and Italian Renaissance touches, but the medley of fountains, terraces and groves is still essentially Arabic *(see pp24–5)*. ◈ Map C3

5 Son Marroig

Perched high above the sea, with its famous Neoclassical gazebo imported from Italy, this L-shaped mansion was fashioned by Archduke Salvador *(see pp20 & 64)*. Much admired in Mallorca, the archduke is remembered here with a museum devoted to his life and collections. In the gardens, you can sit in the white Carrara marble rotunda and gaze at the Na Foradada ("pierced rock") Peninsula, jutting out to sea with an 18-m (59-ft) hole at its centre. ◈ Map C2 • MA-10, south of Deià • 9:30am–2pm & 3–5pm Mon–Sat • Adm

Jardins d'Alfàbia

For more on the public gardens of the Southwest Coast see pp64–5

Left **Deià** Right **Sóller**

Deià

Set in a dramatic ravine that plunges down to the sea, Deià is mostly associated with the English novelist and poet Robert Graves. Settling in the small town in 1929, Graves lived and worked here for the next 56 years, making the place popular with other artists including Picasso and the writer Anaïs Nin. Towering over the town is the modest 18th-century church of Sant Joan Baptista. The adjacent building houses the parish museum; there is also a museum founded by the American archaeologist William Waldren, displaying the prehistory of Mallorca. Hotel La Residencia has attracted many famous guests including Princess Diana and Sir Bob Geldof. ✆ Map C2

Sóller

The town's name reputedly derives from the Arabic *suliar* – "golden bowl" – the valley is famous for its orange groves. Notable buildings include the

Port de Sóller

The French Connection

Before the Sóller Tunnel opened in 1997, the mountain-ringed Sóller Valley was almost cut off from the rest of the island. Thus, the northerly reaches of the island carried out more commerce with France than with Palma. In the 19th century, Sóller enjoyed a brisk orange trade with France, and has never lost its special relationship with the French.

Modernista Banco de Sóller and the Neo-Gothic church of Sant Bartomeu, both the work of a disciple of Antoni Gaudí. Few visitors do more than sit in Plaça Constitució soaking up the atmosphere and sampling tapas, pastries, ice cream and fresh orange juice. The town's vintage electric train provides a superb ride through the mountains to Palma. ✆ Map C2

Port de Sóller

This small resort, set around an excellent natural harbour, has vibrant festivals *(see p52)* and the only beach of any size along the northwestern coast. An atmosphere of low-key chic and family fun prevails. It's the starting point for boat trips along the coast and a good base for walks – a short climb brings you to the Cap Gros lighthouse with its panoramic views *(see also p40)*. ✆ Map C2

9 Fornalutx

This quaint stone village is supremely situated, enjoying a splendid view of towering Puig Major *(see p106)* – Mallorca's highest peak – and of the vast ravine that sweeps down into the valley of orange groves. Silence reigns, except for the lazy sound of goat and sheep bells. The town seems to clutch at its essentially perpendicular setting, with accommodation and dining options making the most of the panorama. You can get here by car, but a better choice is the fragrant hike up from Sóller, passing through the even tinier Biniaraix *(see p98)*. ✆ Map D2

10 Castell d'Alaró

The original castle was built a thousand years ago by the Moors and then refurbished following the "reconquest" by Jaume I in the 13th century. It's little more than rubble now, but the lofty position certainly seems unconquerable enough. At the bottom of the trail is an excellent restaurant; from here you can follow well-beaten paths and dry-stone tracks along the cliff-face *(see also pp54 & 56)*. ✆ Map D3

Fornalutx

A Tour of Dramatic Promontories

Morning

🕙 This drive takes a full day, setting out at 10am or so.

Start at **Andratx** *(see p98)* and take the coast road, MA-10, north. At the point where the road encounters the coastline, you will find the Mirador de Ricardo Roca viewpoint and the **Es Grau** café *(see p80)*. At **Estellencs** *(p98)*, you can also stop for shopping and refreshment.

As the road leaves the town and climbs, there's a stopping point to the left where you can look back at the view. Next stop is the magnificent **Mirador de ses Ànimes** *(p98)*.

At **Banyalbufar** *(p98)*, note the remarkable terraced hillsides. A little way on, you'll see signs for **La Granja** *(pp16–17)*. Head there for lunch and a good look around the mansion and grounds.

Afternoon

After lunch, there's more historic sightseeing at **Valldemossa** *(pp18–21)*, where you can check out the former monastery, museum and old town.

Carrying on north, pop into **Son Marroig** *(p95)* and then wind around into fantastic **Deià**, where you can stop for a stroll.

Continuing on, don't blink or you'll miss Mallorca's smallest village, Lluc-Alcari; and finally, head for the main square in **Sóller**, to have a drink at one of the pleasant cafés, then take the quaint tram down to the **Port de Sóller** for dinner and the rich nightlife.

Left **Mirador de ses Ànimes** Centre **Biniaraix** Right **Orient**

Best of the Rest

1 Port d'Andratx
One of Mallorca's classiest resorts *(see p40)*. ◎ Map A4

2 Andratx
Surrounded by orange and almond trees, which blossom in February, Andratx is a sleepy place that only becomes animated on market day (Wednesday). ◎ Map B4

3 Illa Dragonera
A narrow, rocky island lying at an angle to the coast near Sant Elm. It has been a nature reserve since 1988 and is home to a wide variety of wild flowers and birdlife, including cormorants, Cory's shearwater and the world's largest colony of Eleonora's falcon. According to legend, the Island is visited nightly by dragons. However, its name has more to do with the shape than its popularity with mythical beasts. A rocky path runs between its two headlands, both marked by lighthouses. Ferries from Sant Elm operate in summer, allowing visitors to disembark on the island and explore it for several hours. ◎ Map A4

4 Puigpunyent
Lying in the shadow of Puig de Galatzó, this pretty mountain village is the base for visiting La Reserva nature park. ◎ Map B3

5 Estellencs
Tiny, picturesque mountain town with some restaurants and shops. There's also a rudimentary seaside area around a shingly beach, where the snorkelling is good *(see p50)*. ◎ Map B3

6 Mirador de ses Ànimes
The best mirador (viewpoint) on the entire coast is crowned by the Torre Verger *(see p56)*, which you can climb, just as watchmen did for centuries, keeping a fearful eye out for Saracens and other pirates. ◎ Map B3

7 Banyalbufar
Built by the Moors using dry-stone walls, the town's terraces speak of human ingenuity to create superb farmland out of inhospitable cliffs. There are a few nice hotels, cafés, restaurants, artisan shops and a small, shingly beach. ◎ Map B3

8 Biniaraix
A smaller sibling to Fornalutx *(see p97)*, this adorable village clings to the hill above the Barranc de Biniaraix gorge. ◎ Map C2

9 Bunyola
A charming place in the foot-hills of the Serra de Tramuntana. Inside its church is a much-cherished 14th-century image of the Virgin in alabaster. ◎ Map C3

10 Orient
Those who make the hair-raising road journey from Bunyola to this hamlet at the foot of Puig d'Alfàbia can have a choice of walks including one to Castell d'Alaró *(see pp49, 50 & 56)*. ◎ Map D3

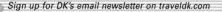

Left **Bar Cubano, Andratx** Right **Cappuccino, Port d'Andratx**

🔟 Cafés and Shops

1 Cooperativa Agrícola Sant Bartomeu, Sóller

This cooperative, founded in 1899, produces four delicious olive oils: soft Mallorquina, fruity Arbequina, spicy Picual and Coupage (a mix of the three others). ◈ *Ctra. de Fornalutx, 8 • 971 630294*

2 Café Açaí, Sóller

Named after a Brazilian fruit known as the "herbal Viagra", this café serves healthy salads and snacks, as well as picnic lunches to take away, and delicious açai juice. ◈ *C/Rectoria, 3 • 971 631818*

3 Bar Roma, Port de Sóller

This traditional bar has been serving locals with drinks and homemade tapas since 1957. There are great views of Soller bay from its seafront terrace. ◈ *Passeig Es Traves, 26 • 971 632223*

4 Jardinería Pedro, Sóller

Row after row of terracotta and painted pottery of all kinds – jars, pots, planters, dishes, bowls, decorative masks and all sorts of hanging containers. It's a wildly colourful place and fun just to roam. ◈ *Carretera Vieja del Puerto, 2*

5 Cappuccino, Port d'Andratx

With a waterfront location by the fishing port, and lovely sunset views, this café serves a range of snacks, sweets, ice cream, soft drinks and cocktails, as well as excellent breakfasts. Free Wi-Fi. ◈ *Avda. Mateu Bosch, 31 • 971 672214*

6 Marianisa, Port d'Andratx

A shop selling fishermen's shirts, swimwear, underwear and accessories. ◈ *Plaza Almirante Oquendo, 7 • 971 671680*

7 Bar Cubano, Andratx

This is where the locals hang out. Inside, you'll find the TV blaring, the usual gambling machines and Mallorcan pottery. ◈ *Plaça Pou, 1 • 971 136367*

8 Ca'n Nadal, Andratx

Founded in 1872, this pastry shop offers such delights as *mantecados* (shortbread), *cremadillo de cabello* (sugar-coated mille feuille), *pastel de chocolate* (iced chocolate cake with walnuts) or *tortaletta rechesol y frutos secos* (moist tart topped with nuts). Also buy a bag of *quelitas* (tiny, egg-shaped crackers). ◈ *C/Juan Carlos I, 7 • 971 136120*

9 Arte Artesanía, Sóller

A jewellery workshop, art gallery and retail outlet, offering contemporary pieces by local artists. Choose from gold, silver, wood, iron or stone pieces. Designs are imaginative and original. ◈ *C/De Sa Lluna, 43 • 971 631732*

10 Brodats Mallorquins, Banyalbufar

Local handmade embroidered items are the speciality, such as tablecloths, baby booties, crocheted doilies and T-shirts. ◈ *C/Baronia, 2 • 971 618236*

Price Categories

For a three-course meal for one with half a bottle of wine (or equivalent meal), taxes and extra charges.	€ under €20
	€€ €20–€30
	€€€ €30–€40
	€€€€ €40–€50
	€€€€€ over €50

Left **Rocamar, Port d'Andratx** Right **Restaurant Villa Italia**

Places to Eat

1 La Gran Tortuga, Peguera

Features a huge deck over the port. The menu includes salmon with curry sauce, grilled squid in its own ink, fillet of veal with clams, crêpes and pear sorbet. ☯ *Aldea Cala Fornells, 1 • Map B4 • 971 686023 • Closed Mon • No dis acc • €€€€*

2 Miramar, Port d'Andratx

The King dines at this central, upmarket place noted for its seafood, fish baked in salt and kobe beef. ☯ *Avda. Mateo Bosch, 18 • Map A4 • 971 671617 • €€€€*

3 Rocamar, Port d'Andratx

Succulent local prawns or fish baked in salt, with *crema catalana* for dessert, are specialities here. The views are fantastic, too. ☯ *Almirante Riera Alemany, 27 • Map A4 • 971 671261 • Mar–Nov • €€€€*

4 Restaurant Villa Italia, Port d'Andratx

Delicious Italian dishes, such as ravioli with porcini mushrooms and panna cotta, and seafood dishes with champagne sauce. The ambience is elegant, and service multilingual. Live music Tuesday and Thursday evenings. ☯ *Camino de San Carlos, 13 • Map A4 • 971 674011 • No dis acc • €€€€€*

5 El Guia, Port de Sóller

Dine on tasty Mallorcan home cooking at this delightful restaurant. Try the stuffed artichokes and for dessert the *gato de almendras* (almond tart). ☯ *C/Castanyer, 2 • Map C2 • 971 630227 • €€€*

6 Es Port, Port de Valldemossa

Get set for seafood salads, a garlicky fish soup, paella, *tumbet* (Mallorcan ratatouille), chicken, pork and their specialities – scorpion fish and bream. Beach-front restaurant with sea and cliff views. ☯ *Map C3 • 971 616194 • No dis acc • €€€*

7 Bens d'Avall, Port de Sóller

Popular restaurant with spectacular mountain and sea views, and memorable Mediterranean and nouvelle cuisine. The melon soup, tuna carpaccio and seafood cannelloni are all wonderful *(see also p82)*. ☯ *Urb. Costa Deià, Carreterra Sóller Deià s/n • Map C2 • 971 632381 • Feb–Oct • €€€€€*

8 Can Toni Moreno, Port d'es Canonge

A classic seafood restaurant serving some of the best paellas on the island. Save room for delicious home-cooked desserts. ☯ *Map B3 • 971 610426 • €€€*

9 Randemar, Port de Sóller

Italian and Mallorcan cuisine served by the sea. The zabaglione is to die for. ☯ *Passeig Es Través, 16 • Map C2 • 971 634578 • Closed Tue • €€€*

10 Ca'n Antuna, Fornalutx

Tasty Mallorcan food, including rabbit, with stunning views from the terrace. The paella is also recommended. ☯ *C/Arbona Colon, 4 • Map D2 • 971 633068 • Closed Sun D, Mon • No dis acc • €€*

Note: Unless otherwise stated, all restaurants have disabled access, accept credit cards and serve vegetarian meals

Left **Port d'Andratx** Right **Bar Deportivo, Fornalutx main square**

Nightclubs and Bars

Gran Casino Mallorca, Urbanizatión Sol de Mallorca, Magaluf

Mallorca's casino offers glitzy bars and clubby salons for a drink between bets *(see p72)*. ◈ *Urb. Sol de Mallorca, end of Andratx motorway (Cala Figuera detour), Magaluf, Calvià • 971 130000*

Barracuda, Port d'Andratx

Revellers of all ages come for the mix of soul, house, hiphop and Spanish music. Wednesday night is Club 21, mostly for German 20-somethings; Thursday is House Party, with guest DJs from Ibiza; Friday is Gay Night; Sunday is Flower Power, with music from the 1960s and 1970s *(see p73)*. ◈ *Centro Commercial Las Velas, local 11 • 971 673606 • Jul–Sep, best from 1am–6am*

Garito Café, Palma

When the café opened in the 1970s it held art exhibitions. In 1998 the bar was turned into a café-club where dance rhythms play well into the night *(see p80)*.

Discoteca Mar Salada, Palma

Classic club playing international and Spanish pop. It's open all weekend from midnight – arrive before 3:30am to avoid queuing. ◈ *Muelle Pelaires, s/n • 971 701271*

Café Central, Sóller

A popular café which gets really busy at dawn. A good place to have a late snack of crusty bread and olive oil and a cocktail or two. Trendy decor. ◈ *Plaça Constitució, 32 • 971 630008*

Discoteca Altamar, Port de Sóller

A large, loud disco for teens and those in their early 20s. Special fiestas include foam parties and tropical nights. ◈ *Corner Es Través and C/Antonio Montis • 971 631205 • 10pm–6am daily to end Sep*

Es Mirall, Port de Sóller

A lively bar with a nice terrace overlooking the bay. There are karaoke nights and local bands occasionally play. ◈ *Camí d'es Far, 21 • 971 634266*

Bar Albatros, Port de Sóller

Full of fishermen exchanging tales in animated Mallorquin. Ask for *una canya* (a beer on tap). ◈ *C/ Marina, 48 • 8pm–1am*

The Asgard, Port de Sóller

A pleasant Irish pub just a few steps away from the beach, serving real Irish beers. There's a terrace with sea views, and a big screen for sports fans. ◈ *Passeig Es Través, 15 • 971 631524*

Bar Deportivo, Fornalutx

The main square in town is full of seating for several bars. This one is on the corner; others include Café Sa Plaça and Café Ca'n Benet. Locals and foreign visitors mingle till the early hours. ◈ *C/La Plaça, 1*

For more good places to eat on the Southwest Coast see p82; *Many nightclubs and bars are open only during the summer*

Left **Statue, Lluc** Centre **City gate, Alcúdia** Right **Ruin, Península de Formentor**

North Coast

AS DIFFERENT EUROPEAN NATIONALITIES *have laid holiday claim to various parts of the island, this northernmost corner* has developed a certain English-Scottish-Irish character. (That's not to say you won't encounter German, French, Scandinavian, Dutch and Italian visitors, too.) It's a mountainous area, and where those jagged cliffs meet the sea you'll find some of Mallorca's loveliest coves and bays. Add ancient sites and flamboyant festivals to the mix, and its obvious why many people take pleasure in exploring this region.

Statue,
Alcúdia

🔟 Sights

1. Gorg Blau
2. Cala Tuent
3. Monestir de Nostra Senyora de Lluc
4. Pollença
5. Ermita de Nostra Senyora del Puig
6. Cala Sant Vicenç
7. Port de Pollença
8. Península de Formentor
9. Alcúdia and Port d'Alcúdia
10. Parc Natural de S'Albufera

Reservoir, Gorg Blau

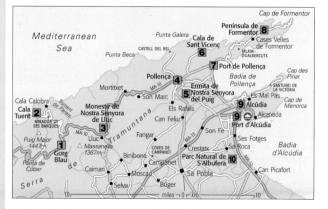

Monestir de Nostra Senyora de Lluc

cultures, combine to create a peaceful, inviting atmosphere for believers and non-believers alike. You can stay in the monastery's comfortable rooms, and explore the ancient mysteries of the surrounding area *(see also pp26–7).* ✎ Map D2

1 Gorg Blau

Heading out of Sóller, on the way to Lluc, the C710 is perhaps the most dramatic drive of all, traversing tunnels and gorges on its way between Puig Major and Puig Massanella. This beautiful but bleak ravine has been known since ancient times, as evidenced by the Talayot pillar that has been left as a silent sentinel. Several reservoirs have been created nearby *(see also p36).* ✎ Map D2

2 Cala Tuent

A side turn off the road to Sa Calobra leads its winding way down to Cala Tuent, a small cove with a beach and a 13th-century church, Ermita de Sant Llorenç. Cala Tuent is probably the quietest beach on the northern coast, and there's a nice café-restaurant on the far side of the cove. Swimming here is safe as long as you don't venture out too far *(see also p42).* ✎ Map D2

3 Monestir de Nostra Senyora de Lluc

Since time immemorial, long before the existence of Christianity, this spot has been Mallorca's holiest pilgrimage point. The heady mountain air and the presence of many groves of oak trees, considered sacred in Neolithic and ancient

4 Pollença

Founded by the Romans in the foothills of the Serra de Tramuntana, Pollença still has much of its old-world charm with narrow, twisting streets, some good restaurants and a lively Sunday market. There's a great municipal museum, too *(see p63)*, while the pride of the town is the beautiful Way of the Cross, leading to a chapel that houses a Gothic statue of Christ. Climbing the seemingly endless set of steps (365 in all), you pass the Stations of the Cross. The statue is carried around town on Good Friday, in a moving torchlight procession. ✎ Map E1

Calvari staircase, Pollença

Cala Sant Vicenç

5 Ermita de Nostra Senyora del Puig

As with all of Mallorca's religious retreats, it's the serenity of age-less isolation that rewards. Though located only a one-hour walk from atmospheric Pollença, it feels like you're a world away from modern life, on this modest bump of a hill, barely 300 m (984 ft) high. Over the centuries, the typically tawny-hued stone complex has been home to both nuns and monks, but now, although still Church property, only overnight guests use the cubicles *(see p146)*. A well-laid dry-stone path leads the way, the air redolent with wild herbs and the pungent smell of rural life, the arid land-scape broken up with olive, carob and fig trees, and dashes of oleander and wildflowers *(see also p60)*. Map E2

6 Cala Sant Vicenç

The resort has poss-ibly the clearest, most beautiful blue waters of any truly sandy beach on the island yet is rarely overcrowded. There are actually three *calas* (coves) – Cala Sant Vicenç, Cala Barques and Cala Molins – separated by rocky outcroppings. Cala Molins is accessed down a steep hill from the main part of the resort

Mallorca's Heights

The Serra de Tramuntana runs for 88 km (55 miles) from Andratx to Pollença. Its highest peaks, between Sóller and Lluc, are Puig Major (1,447 m/4,747 ft) and Puig Massanella (1,367 m/ 4,485 ft). Explore the mountains on foot if you can, so as to smell wild rose-mary, listen to sheep bells, breathe in pure air and marvel at pine trees growing out of red rocks.

and has the most laid-back character, as well as a broader beach than the others *(see also p42)*. Map E1

7 Port de Pollença

The port is a major resort *(see p41)*, with beautiful restau-rants, unique shops, a lovely pedestrian-only zone right along the water and loads of nightlife. It is a favourite with families year-round, while older visitors flock in winter. A large commu-nity of foreign residents, mostly retired British, have made it their permanent home. Map E1

Península de Formentor

Church, Alcúdia

8 Península de Formentor

Mallorca's wildest part is full of vivid vistas and precipitous plunges, where driving or hiking are exhilarating and unforgettable experiences. It is also home to Mallorca's most venerable hotel, where movie stars have hobnobbed, and where crowned heads and diplomats have decided the fate of nations (see pp28–9). ✎ Map F1

9 Alcúdia and Port d'Alcúdia

This two-part municipality consists of Mallorca's most striking medieval town (see pp30–31) uneasily conjoined with one of its brashest tourist ports (see p41). The area around the fishing harbour is the most attractive, with the broad promenade of Passeig Maritim facing a row of fish restaurants. ✎ Map F2

10 Parc Natural de S'Albufera

The wetland south of Port d'Alcúdia was once a swamp, most of which was drained in the 1860s. The remaining marshes, overgrown with reeds, can be explored via marked trails. A major conservation project, this is an excellent place for bird-watching (see also p37). ✎ Map F2

Parc Natural de S'Albufera

A Stroll Around Historic Pollença

Mid-Morning

🕐 Beginning at about 10am on any day but Monday, this walk around **Pollença** (see p103) should take three to four hours.

Start on the southern side of town, with a visit to the **Museu Municipal de Pollença** (p63) and the beautiful building that houses it – the convent, church and cloister of Sant Domingo, now entirely given over to civic cultural purposes. (It is closed on Mondays.)

Walk north a couple of blocks and pop into **Antik I Art** a wonderful antiques shop. From here, continue up to the Plaça Mayor and admire the Modernista architecture of the Hotel Juma and the marvellous rose window tracery of the **Nostra Senyora dels Àngels** parish church (see p58).

Early Afternoon

Now walk up the left side of the church until you get to **Aquamarina** (p107) with its unusual handcrafted jewellery, and then stop off at the **Café del Calvari** (p107) for refreshment before striding up the famous cypress-lined Calvari steps.

Finally, head down Les Creus and Gruat streets to the picturesque Pont Romà, a bridge thought by some to be from ancient Roman times, but probably dating from the Middle Ages.

After your tour, have lunch at either the interesting **La Tetera** (p108) or the famous **La Fonda** (p83).

Left **Sa Calobra** Centre **Coves de Campanet** Right **Santuari de la Victòria**

📖🔟 Best of the Rest

1 Puig Major
Jutting skyward like a stony crown, this majestic mountain is flanked on one side by the Sóller Valley, with its picturesque villages, and on the other by Lluc and the tranquil valley of Aubarca (see also box on p104). ✎ Map D2

2 Mirador de Ses Barques
Located at the top of the road that leads down to Sa Calobra (entry 3), this marvellous viewpoint overlooks the skein of road loops and, beyond all of the rocky outcroppings, the sea. Stop for refreshment at the restaurant here. ✎ Map D2

3 Sa Calobra
A rapturously beautiful bay, which explains why the tourist buses pour in by the dozen every day. The journey via the steep, winding road is also memorable (see p49). An easier approach is by boat from Port de Sóller, passing isolated bays and with great views of Puig Major. ✎ Map D2

4 Torrent de Pareis
Walk through a tunnel from Sa Calobra to reach the Torrent de Pareis, which begins in the mountains at the confluence of the torrents of Lluc and Gorg. This canyon is the second largest in the Mediterranean, and the point at which it exits into the sea is spectacular. However, hiking in the canyon can be dangerous, especially after rain (see p36). ✎ Map D2

5 Castell del Rei
A popular walk leads to this remote, abandoned mountain castle north of Pollença (see pp54 & 56). ✎ Map E1 • 971 530801 (walk by prior request only)

6 Mirador de Mal Pas
This viewpoint is the first stop on a tour of the Península de Formentor (see p28). ✎ Map F1

7 Hotel Barcélo Formentor
Argentine visionary Adán Diehl's contribution to high-end island tourism has had its ups and downs but is currently riding high again (see p141). ✎ Map F1

8 Santuari (Ermita) de la Victòria
Built in 1678, the church is as much fortress as spiritual centre due to pirate raids in that era. It houses a revered icon and a vibrant Baroque altarpiece. ✎ Map F1

9 Cap des Pinar
Much of the cape is a restricted military zone, but you can take in the view from the terrace of the Mirador del Victòria, walk to the ruins of the Talaia d'Alcúdia or climb Penya Roja. ✎ Map F1

10 Coves de Campanet
A cave complex with a lake and the thinnest stalactite on record. The tour lasts 45 minutes and is less crowded than others. ✎ C713, 16 km (10 miles) SW of Alcúdia • Map E2 • 971 516130 • Apr–Sep: 10am–7pm; Oct–Mar: 10am–6pm • Adm

Left **Café S'Illa** Centre **Galeries Vincenç** Right **Arrels**

⟨₀⟩10 Cafés and Shops

1 Café del Calvari, Pollença
Light snacks, such as tapas, *pa amb oli (see p78)*, gazpacho, salads and strawberries and cream. ⊗ *Pl. Martorell (at the bottom of the Calvari staircase) • 971 532693*

2 Bar Mallorca, Cala S. Vicenç
On the beach, look for the little stone hut with red tile roof and dried grasses over its terrace. Open late for drinks and snacks. ⊗ *Cala Molins, Cala Sant Vicenç • 971 534603*

3 Aquamarina, Pollença
A jewellery shop offering precious and semi-precious stones set in silver and gold. All designs are original, some using unusual stones, such as the "rose of the Incas", purple sugilites, and Alexandrite sapphires. ⊗ *C/Virgen del Carmen, 15 • 917 866890*

4 Ceràmiques Monti-Sion, Pollença
A traditional ceramics workshop with beautiful reproduction tiles and also a collection of antique originals from the 18th and 19th centuries. ⊗ *C/Monti-Sion, 19*

5 La Tetera, Pollença
A friendly little café, open all day, serving delicious coffee, a wide variety of teas, light snacks and even cream teas. More substantial fare on the eclectic menu includes Thai green curry, goat's cheese salad and Spanish-style sandwiches. ⊗ *C/Temple, 8 • 971 530792*

6 Galeries Vicenç, Pollença
Two large floors full of Mallorcan crafts and original art. You'll find traditional *robes de llengües* cloth, genuine antiques, lamps, sculpture, rustic furniture, wooden bowls, ceramics and glassware. ⊗ *Can Berenguer Roundabout (Rotonda) • 971 530450 • www.teixitsvicens.com*

7 Café L'Algar, Port de Pollença
A *croissanteria* with style and a sense of history, tricked out in green awnings and matching director's chairs, with beaux-arts lamps and potted plants. ⊗ *Plaça Miquel Capllonch, 5 • 971 866880*

8 Gelats Valls, Pollença
Milk, eggs, sugar and fresh local fruits are the ingredients the Valls family have been using since the 1930s to make some of the best ice cream on the island. ⊗ *C/Canonge Rotger, 2 • 971 530264*

9 Arrels, Port de Pollença
An amazing array of handmade Mallorcan crafts, some of it the island's best. The traditional ceramic whistles are featured, as well as olive-wood carvings, and a special line of leather masks by Calimba of Palma. ⊗ *Passeig Saralegui, 54 • 971 867017*

10 Café S'Illa, Port d'Alcúdia
This sophisticated café with touches of Modernista is always thronged with people. Smartly dressed waiters set the tone. ⊗ *Passeig Marítim, 8*

Left **Stay** Right **Ca'l Patró**

Price Categories

For a three-course meal for one with half a bottle of wine (or equivalent meal), taxes and extra charges.

€	under €20
€€	€20–€30
€€€	€30–€40
€€€€	€40–€50
€€€€€	over €50

🔟 Places to Eat

1 Iru, Port de Pollença

This family-run seafront restaurant has a lovely terrace with harbour views. It serves creative Mallorcan cuisine with an Italian influence. ◈ *Passeig Anglada Camarassa, 23 • 971 867002 • Closed Dec–Jan, Tue in winter • €€€*

2 Stay, Port de Pollença

Upmarket restaurant serving some of the best cuisine on the island. Fish is the speciality, but the menu of new international fare is huge. Good value lunch menu. ◈ *Main jetty • 971 864013 • www.stayrestaurant.com • €€€€€*

3 Bodega d'es Port, Port d'Alcudia

Antiques, wooden beams and a terrace with sea views provide the setting for traditional tapas, paella and excellent seafood. ◈ *C/Teodoro Canet, 8 • 971 549633 • Closed Nov–Dec • No dis acc • €*

4 Clivia, Pollença

Authentic Mallorcan cuisine in an elegant, colonial setting. Don't miss the fish baked in salt crust or the fig and biscuit ice cream. ◈ *Avda. Pollèntia, 5–7 • 971 534616 • Closed Sun • €€€€*

5 Es Guix, Escorca

This old stone country house set amid oak groves and beside a lake, offers traditional fare such as roast kid and snails. ◈ *Between Caimari and Monestir de Nostra Senyora de Lluc • 971 517092 • www.esguix.com • Open Mar–Dec: Wed–Mon, L only • €€€*

6 La Balada del Agua del Mar, Port de Pollença

Set in a beautiful house with Modernist touches and a lush garden setting in front of the water. The select menu changes regularly and features typical Mallorcan specialties. ◈ *Passeig Voramar, 5 • 971 864276 • Closes early; reservations essential • Closed Nov–Mar • €€€€*

7 Ca'n Cuarassa, Port de Pollença

Set in a handsomely restored mansion in extensive gardens, this restaurant offers Mallorcan and international specialities including succulent meats grilled over charcoal. ◈ *Platja Ca'n Cuarassa • 971 864266 • €€€€*

8 Ca'l Patró, Cala Sant Vicenç

A lovely terrace restaurant overlooking a beautiful cove. Shy away from the hot dogs and pizzas in favour of the local dishes. ◈ *Cala Barques • 971 533899 • Jan–mid-Mar; Closed Tue • No dis acc • €€*

9 Los Zarzales, Port de Pollença

Mallorcan food is served with an original flair, such as cod with honey and *sobrassada*. ◈ *C/Jafuda Cresques, 11 • 971 865137 • €€€*

10 Es Canyar, Alcúdia

This mediterranean-style restaurant features a lovely interior garden, live music and an ever-changing menu of unique dishes. ◈ *C/Major, 2 • 971 547282 • €€€*

Note: *Unless otherwise stated, all restaurants have disabled access, accept credit cards and serve vegetarian dishes*

Left **Maremar Beach Club** Right **Menta**

🔟 Nightclubs and Bars

1 La Birreria, Polleça
This central bar serves a wide range of international and Spanish beers, as well as tapas. A huge blackboard behind the counter lists the specials of the day. ✪ C/Colón, 3 • Closed Mon

2 Pub El Convent, Alcúdia
One of the few places in which to enjoy a drink and listen to good music in downtown Alcúdia. ✪ Jaume Roig, s/n

3 The Nag's Head, Port de Pollença
Open from noon until late, this bar is only a 2 minute walk away from the main beach. You can enjoy a drink in the beer garden or catch up on news and sport in the satellite TV lounge. ✪ C/Almirant Cervera, 200

4 Magic Disco, Port d'Alcúdia
Hosting some of the island's craziest parties, Magic has two floors topped by a glass pyramid. The top-level dance floor has excellent views, and there's also a chill-out terrace. ✪ Avda. Tucán • May–Oct & weekends in winter

5 Skau Disco, Ca'n Picafort
One of the oldest discos in Mallorca, Skau was founded in the 1960s. It is famous for its foam parties but has quieter areas too, for the less energetic clients. ✪ Avda. José Trias, 14 • May–Oct & weekends in winter

6 Chivas, Port de Pollença
The crowd is young; the place is loud and dark, featuring mirrors and a glass ceiling with a state-of-the-art lighting system over the dance floor (see also p73). ✪ C/Metge Llopis, 5 • May–Oct: 11pm–6am daily (Nov–Apr: Fri–Sat only) • Adm

7 14:40 Café-Club, Pollença
One of the busiest venues in the area, 14:40 has a varied and interesting programme of live gigs and DJs. ✪ Miquel Bota Totxo, 6 • Closed Mon

8 Maremar Beach Club, Port d'Alcúdia
Decorated in a white, minimalist style with huge glass windows, Maremar has a lovely terrace overlooking the sea. Try one of their delicious cocktails. ✪ Avda. del Mar, 8, Playa de Muro

9 Menta, Port d'Alcúdia
Done up like a lavish Roman villa, with terraces, fountains and even a swimming pool, Menta is one of the best clubs in Mallorca. Party night themes include Latin, African and Roman Toga (see also p73). ✪ Avda. Tucan • 971 893257 • 11pm–6:30am • Adm

10 Shamrock, Port d'Alcúdia
A popular Irish pub located in the port. It holds varied live music events every night, and is also a good place to watch sports on TV. ✪ C/Torreta, 3

➤ Following pages **Bunyola**

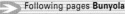

Left **Ses Paisses** Centre **Cala Figuera** Right **Mondragó**

Southeast Coast

THIS IS BEACH COUNTRY PAR EXCELLENCE!
While some of the beaches have seen the worst of mass tourism, more remain as beautiful as ever, offering some of the Mediterranean's most clear, azure and inviting waters. Here, too, you'll find the verdant Serra de Llevant mountain range and some of the island's best natural parks, not to mention its most important ancient sites and most magical caves waiting to be explored.

Statue, Santuari de Sant Salvador

 Sights

1	Capdepera
2	Ses Paisses
3	Coves d' Artà
4	Coves d'es Hams
5	Coves del Drac
6	Santuari de Sant Salvador
7	Parc Natural de Mondragó
8	Cala Figuera
9	Capocorb Vell
10	Illa de Cabrera

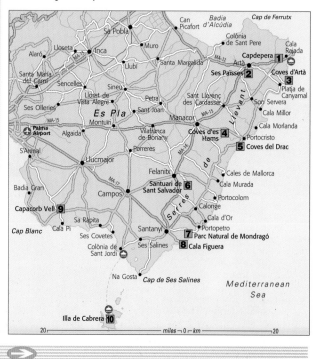

Castell de Capdepera

Capdepera
You can glimpse this castle from miles away, its rickrack form sprawling appealingly around the crest of its sizeable hill. A citadel of some sort has existed here since Roman times, guarding the sea approach, but the present crenellated classic dates back to King Sanç in the 14th century. You can drive up, if you're lucky enough to find the right street in the tightly knit little town below, but the walk up from pleasant Plaça de l'Orient is far more fun. Within the walls is a curious little Gothic church, from the flat roof of which you can take in more spectacular vistas. ✎ *Map H3*

Ses Païsses
A link with the Mallorcans of some 3,000 years ago, these Bronze Age ruins of a Talayot village include a massive Cyclopean portal *(see p55)* formed from three stone slabs weighing up to eight tons each. Inside are several rooms and a watchtower; and the settlement is surrounded by a drystone wall. ✎ *South of Artà • Map G3 • Apr–Oct: 10am–12:30pm, 2:30–6:30pm Mon–Sat; Nov–Mar: 9am–12:30pm, 2–5pm Mon–Fri • Adm*

Coves d'Artà
During the Christian Conquest, Jaume I found 2,000 Arabs hiding with their cattle in this unusual network of caves. However, it was not until 1876, when geologist Edouard Martel entered the grottoes, 46 m (151 ft) above the sea at Cap Vermell, that they were studied. Another early visitor was Jules Verne, whose book *Journey to the Centre of the Earth* is said to have been inspired by them *(see also p45)*. ✎ *Ctra. de las Cuevas, Capdepera • Map H3 • 971 841293 • 10am–5pm daily (to 6pm May–Oct) • Adm*

Coves d'es Hams
These caves are less interesting than the Coves del Drac or Coves d'Artà. Their name means "fishhooks", which the stalactites are said to resemble. You get a guided tour and a concert *(see also p45)*. ✎ *Ctra. Portocristo–Manacor • Map G4 • www.cuevas-hams.com • Apr–Oct: 10am–6pm; Nov–Mar: 10:30am–5pm • 971 820988 • Adm*

Coves d'Artà

5 Coves del Drac

Mallorca's most spectacular cave system is beautifully lit and can be toured in a gondola-style boat *(see pp32–3)*. ✪ Map G4

Cala Figuera

6 Santuari de Sant Salvador

The castle-like structure stands 4 km (2 miles) east of Felanitx, on top of Puig Sant Salvador, the highest mountain of the Serres de Llevant. Founded in the 14th century, and remodelled in the 18th century, the sanctuary is an important place of pilgrimage. The view includes the south-eastern coast of Mallorca. As in other former monasteries, visitors are allowed to stay in basic rooms *(see p146)*. ✪ Puig de Sant Salvador, Felanitx • Map F5 • 971 827282

7 Parc Natural de Mondragó

Marked as a protected area in 1992, the park incorporates marshes, rocky coasts, beaches, dunes, farmland, pine forest and scrub. Country lanes and easy trails provide access. Look out for herons, egrets, puffins, coots, ducks, finches and rabbits. ✪ South of Portopetro • Map F6 • Visitor Centre, Ses Fonts den'Alis: 971 181022

Containing Mass Tourism

Mass tourism is now confined to parts of the island where it encroached in the 1960s, primarily Cala Millor and some of the Cales de Mallorca. Other areas, most notably the prototype Cala d'Or, have been developed in a more sensitive way, favouring Spanish architectural styles – a pleasant mix of Andalusian and Balearic, with a hint of North African.

---

8 Cala Figuera

This tiny old fishing hamlet is an underdeveloped gem. It probably owes its survival to the simple fact that it has no beach, the closest one being 4 km (2 miles) away at Cala Santanyí. What it does have is pleasant low-rise structures and an array of eateries and people-watching cafés. The fishing harbour is part of a fjord-like bay. ✪ Map F6

Santuari de Sant Salvador

Talaiotic ruins, Capocorb Vell

Capocorb Vell

⁹ This Talayot settlement was probably established around 1000 BC. Originally, it consisted of five stone structures *(talaiots)* and 28 smaller dwellings. The amazing Cyclopean walls, reaching 4 m (13 ft) in places, would have served as protection, but little more is known about the function of the rooms or the lives of the ancient inhabitants. Be sure to have a drink at the visitors' bar, which is like something out of *The Flintstones*. ⊗ *Ctra. MA–6014 Llucmajor–Cap Blanc, km 23 • Map D5 • 10am–4:30pm daily exc Thu • Adm*

Illa de Cabrera

¹⁰ Cabrera ("Goat Island") lies 18 km (11 miles) off the mainland. A rocky, bare place and virtually uninhabited, it nevertheless has a rich history. It served as a prison camp during the Napoleonic War and was used as a base by Barbary pirates. Boat trips leave from Colònia de Sant Jordi and take a day – highlights include a 14th-century castle on the island *(see p57)* and Cova Blava *(see p45)*. Keep an eye out for the rare Lilford's lizard, identifiable by its dog-like face. ⊗ *Park information office: Plaça Espanya, Palma • 971 725010; Boat excursions: C/Explanada del Port, Colònia de Sant Jordi • Map H6 • 971 649034 • Excursions daily at 9:30am • Adm*

Five Seaside Beauties

Morning

🕐 This itinerary, incorporating driving and walking, will take a full day.

Set out in the morning at lovely **Porto Cristo** *(see p116)*, with its terrace café-restaurants overlooking the port's palisades. Pop into **Autèntic Mallorca** *(p117)* and be sure to buy some Mallorcan chocolate and other local products.

Bypassing the infamously overdeveloped Cales de Mallorca, **Portocolom** *(p116)* is next, perhaps the most unspoiled and seductively beautiful fishing village left on the island. Be sure to check out the painted façades of the old town, and walk up to the colourful **Bar Els Tamarells** *(p119)* for a drink and to admire the sleepy central square.

Afternoon

Make your way down to **Portopetro**, a minuscule port that's lost none of its authenticity. Have lunch at **El Campo** *(p118)* just out of town on the road to Alquería Blanca.

Cala Figuera is further south. Stroll around its woods-encircled harbour and browse around the gift shops.

On the western side of the Cap de ses Salines, you'll find **Colònia de Sant Jordi**, a rangy beach town with a bright, relaxing port. Stop here to have a wonderful fresh fish dinner at **Port Blau** *(p118)*, and maybe spend the night at the quaint **Hostal Playa** *(p144)*.

Left **Cala Rajada** Centre **Porto Cristo** Right **Cala d'Or**

🔟 Best of the Rest

1 Artà
Ancient, prosperous town noted for its basketry. ◈ *Map G3*

2 Cala Rajada
This fishing port on Mallorca's eastern tip, surrounded by fine beaches and pretty coves, is a crowded resort in summer *(see p41)*. ◈ *Map H3*

3 Castell de Santueri
Artà's crowning glory is its hilltop fortress, the view from which is one of Mallorca's most characteristic sights: a jumble of tiles in every shade of brown.

4 Porto Cristo
A family resort at the end of a sheltered inlet. The nearby Coves del Drac *(see pp32–3)* and aquarium *(see p33)* are popular with day-trippers. ◈ *Map G4*

5 Felanitx
The town is at the centre of a wine-producing area and also known for its floral-decorated pottery and its capers, or "green pearls", which you can buy at the Sunday market. ◈ *Map F5*

6 Portocolom
This attractive fishing village was named in honour of Christopher Columbus, who is said (without much evidence) to have been born here. It has found a new lease of life as a resort favoured by Spanish visitors. ◈ *Map G5*

7 Cala d'Or
Not just one cove, but many, with their respective beaches and pueblo-style villas, make up this garden-green, stylish zone. Each former humble fishing dock has metamorphosed into a classy marina catering for a discerning set of international clientele. ◈ *Map F5*

8 Santanyí
This is the café centre for all the foreigners who own villas nearby, but it's still very Spanish. Buildings are made from the same golden sandstone used in Palma's cathedral. The streets near the church are the focus of a lively Wednesday market. ◈ *Map F6*

9 Campos
A famous painting by 17th-century Sevillian artist Murillo hangs in the parish church of this dusty agricultural town. Next door is a museum with a collection of offertory bowls. ◈ *Map E5*

10 Ses Covetes
These days there's no trace of the "small caves", presumed ancient Roman burial niches, that inspired the name. Located at the northern end of Es Trenc *(see p43)*, the island's finest, longest, totally undeveloped, clothing-optional beach, this place resembles more of a dusty shanty-town than anything else. ◈ *Map E6*

Church interior, Artà

For public gardens near the Southeast Coast see p65

Around the Island – Southeast Coast

Left **Bar Marítimo** Centre **Café Sa Plaça** Right **Sa Pedra**

Cafés and Shops

1 Bar Marítimo, Cala Rajada
Looks a bit like the deck of an ocean liner. It's a place to relax, have a drink or a snack, and survey the busy boats going in and out. ◈ *Passeig Marítim • 971 738192*

2 Sa Pedra, Porto Cristo
Café-restaurant hung with contemporary paintings and with a huge terrace overlooking the palisades, boats and port. Ice creams, snacks and full meals available *(see p81)*. ◈ *C/ Verí, 4 • 971 820932*

3 Café 3, Cala Rajada
Overlooking the marina, this light and airy bar with balconies and spacious, decked outdoor areas, giving it a beach house feel. There is live music on Tuesday and Friday nights. ◈ *Avenida America s/n • 971 565356*

4 Komudus, Porto Cristo
A shop with original designs from Menorca: suede bags, traditional shoes and sandals, original T-shirts and fine linen clothing. They also sell anodized aluminium jewellery. ◈ *C/Mar, 27 • 971 821527*

5 Autèntic Mallorca, Porto Cristo
This special shop has all things Mallorcan: some 90 products including sandals, natural scents, dolls, musical instruments, glass, preserves, sausages, liqueurs, *turrón* (nougat), fig confections and olives. ◈ *C/Sant Jordi, 18 • 971 821108*

6 Café Sa Plaça, Santanyí
Come for *pa amb oli (see p78)*, olives, ham, pickled peppers and Mallorcan cheeses. The refurbished interior has marble tabletops and archways, and outside you can watch the local action in the main square *(see p81)*. ◈ *Plaça Major, 26 • 971 653278*

7 Reina Rana, Santanyí
A treasure trove of glittering costume jewellery, beautiful textiles for the home and hundreds of original gift ideas. ◈ *Plaça Major 15 • 971 642075*

8 Basketry Shops, Artà
Artà is famous as Mallorca's centre for handsome everyday items made from the tough fibres of the *palmito* (palmetto) plant, which grows wild all over the island. ◈ *Miguel Fuster, C/Pep Not, 16; and Aina Alzamora, C/Parres, 20*

9 Panaderia Pons, Colònia de Sant Jordi
The *ensaimades* (spiral-shaped sweet pastries) are light and fluffy and are sold alongside other delicious local pastries and various picnic essentials. ◈ *C/Major, 20 • 971 655171*

10 Toca Madera, Colònia de Sant Jordi
Toca Madera stocks cotton clothes and unusual gift items from all over world, including candles, glassware, masks and sandals. ◈ *C/Estanys, 4; C/Gabriel Roca, 5*

Price Categories

For a three-course meal for one with half a bottle of wine (or equivalent meal), taxes and extra charges.	€ under €20
	€€ €20–€30
	€€€ €30–€40
	€€€€ €40–€50
	€€€€€ over €50

Left **Portopetro** Right **L'Arcada**

Places to Eat

1 S'Assecador, Porto Cristo
Decorated with Moroccan tilework and pictures of old Mallorca. Enjoy a view of the marina while you partake of a traditional Mallorcan meal. ◈ C/ Mar, 11 • 971 820826 • Closed Thu • €€€

2 Molí d'en Sopa, Porto Cristo-Manacor
Close to a windmill on the crest of a hill. The skate salad is unusual, or try the chicken breast stuffed with salmon, and plantains flambé for dessert. ◈ Ctra. Manacor-Porto Cristo, km 4 • 971 550193 • €€€€€

3 Sa Cuina, Portocolom
The food here combines traditional Mallorcan dishes and modern international cuisine. The decor is a nice mix of traditional and contemporary design. ◈ Ctra. s'Horta-Portocolom, C/Vapor de Santueri s/n • 971 824 080 • Closed Thu & Jan • €€€

4 Es Molí d'en Bou, Sa Coma
A Michelin-starred restaurant with a warm, modern design, offering three fixed-price tasting menus of creative Mallorcan cuisine. The "chef's table" in the kitchen seats up to eight, for a memorable dining experience. ◈ Hotel Protur Biomar, C/Liles • 971 569663 • www.esmolidenbou.es • €€€€€

5 Ca'n Martina, Portopetro
Come for fresh fish and Mallorcan specialities including black paella, as well as kids' standards such as burgers. ◈ C/ Cristóbal Colóm N, 56 • 971 657517 • €€

6 El Campo, between Alquería Blanca and Portopetro
The tantalizing aromas are the first things you'll notice, then the infectious Spanish music. Regional dishes include roasted peppers, grilled meat, fish and rice soup and barbecued rabbit. ◈ Carretera de Portopetro, 44 • 971 164265 • €€€

7 L'Arcada, Cala Figuera
Has the most central spot on the port, with the best views. Fresh fish dishes depend on the day's catch. Also pizza, vegetable dishes and Mallorcan food. ◈ Calle Virgen del Carmen, 80 • 971 645032 • €€

8 Port Blau, Colònia de Sant Jordi
Uses fish caught around Illa de Cabrera, served up in vast portions in an open dining area on the port. ◈ C/Gabriel Roca, 67 • 971 656555 • Closed Tue & Dec–Jan • €€€

9 Celler Sa Sinia, Felanitx
Chef Biel Perelló is a local legend: his delicious seafood-based menu has made Sa Sinia one of the best restaurants on the island. Try the lobster stew. ◈ C/Pescadors, 25 • 971 824323 • Closed Sun • €€€

10 Sa Canova, Campos
Good country fare: Mallorcan soup of cabbage and pork, grilled rabbit in onion sauce with snails or roast duck in port with fresh apple and orange slices. ◈ Avda. Ronda Estacion, 35 • 971 650210 • Closed Sun dinner, Mon • €€€

Note: Unless otherwise stated, all restaurants have disabled access, accept credit cards and serve vegetarian meals

Cala d'Or

🔟 Nightclubs and Bars

1 Café Parisien, Artà
A wonderfully rustic place, with an open fireplace, two dogs and an affable proprietor. There are drinks (including drinking chocolates), pastries, tapas and daily specials. ✆ *C/Ciutat, 18 • 971 835440*

2 Physical, Cala Ratjada
The port attracts a young, active crowd for whom this is the numero uno club in town, leading the way with techno, hip-hop and black music. ✆ *C/Coconar, 17 • www.grupo-physical.com*

3 Twist, Porto Cristo
A hip place done up in primary colours, with tiny halogen lights above a granite bar and an assemblage by Basque artist S'Anto Iñorrieta. ✆ *Es Riuet • 971 820173*

4 Es Carreró, Porto Cristo
This entire street, just a block from the Marina, is loaded with tiny dives that are thronged from midnight to 6am. Glitzily-dressed young people come out to party in Makoki's, Saltre Pub, Pub Limite, Wall Street, Séstil, Es Bidò and more *(see p73).*

5 Bar Els Tamarells, Portocolom
Look for the drunk-looking seahorse sign. Inside, it's loud and packed with young Spaniards and Mallorcans. The main room has a big TV, bar and tables, while the terrace has views of the entire port. There is also a quieter room with table football. ✆ *C/Mar, 21 • 971 825384*

6 Café La Playa Chill Out, Porto Colom
A cool and relaxing terrace-bar by the beach with, as the name suggests, a chilled-out vibe. International DJs play Nu Jazz. ✆ *Porto Colom beach*

7 Bolero Disco, Cala Ratjada
A glamorously appointed discotheque in the heart of Cala Ratjada. DJs play pop and dance music, and there's live music most nights, as well. ✆ *C/Leonor Servera, 36 • www.bolero-angels.com*

8 Port Pub, Port de Cala d'Or
The evocative decor mixes US license plates and nautical objects. The annex below is the El Faro wine bar, and all of it is part of a white stucco complex of trendy shops and restaurants. ✆ *Avda. Cala Llonga, Port Petit • 971 659006*

9 Noah's Café, Cala Ratjada
On the harbour, with amazing views, Noah's serves healthy food from early morning, and excellent cocktails until late at night. A relaxed atmosphere and great music. ✆ *Avda. América, 1–2 • 971 818125 • www.cafenoahs.com*

10 Disco Mond-Bar, Cala Figuera
A very popular spot with a huge terrace, Miró-esque decorations and a good-sized dance floor. Music tends towards hits of the day, with occasional live acts. ✆ *C/Pintor Bernareggi*

Left **Els Calderers** Centre **Petra** Right **Characteristic windmills on the Central Plain**

Central Plain

YOU HAVEN'T REALLY SEEN MALLORCA *until you've wended your way over Es Pla (The Plain). People argue whether the mountains or coast represents the real Mallorca, but the true heart of the island is surely to be found in the villages here, which make few concessions to tourism. This is where food is grown and where most of the island's leatherworkers, potters and the manufacturers of traditional robes de llengües (cloth of flame) and the prized artificial pearls are based.*

🔟 Sights

1. Binissalem
2. Lloseta
3. Inca
4. Sa Pobla
5. Muro
6. Petra
7. Manacor
8. Els Calderers
9. Montuïri
10. Gordiola Glassworks

Gordiola Glassworks

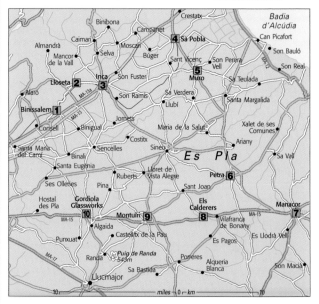

1 Binissalem

Don't be put off by its brutal appearance from the highway. Hidden behind the commercial tackiness, the historic centre dates back to the ancient Romans, and is now dominated by centuries-old stone mansions very much

Church, Binissalem

worth a stroll around. The town's wealth arose from its pre-eminence as the island's wine producer, starting 500 years ago. In recent years, after a century or so of decline, its reputation has again been on the rise, as evidenced by the important winery outlets along the main road *(see pp51 & 124)*. ✪ *Map D3*

2 Lloseta

Traditionally part of the leather-crafting enterprises in the area, this town is situated on a sloping foothill. It has a pleasant, tree-lined approach, a charming central square and several good restaurants. ✪ *Map D3*

3 Inca

Inca, one of the last stops on the train journey from Palma, is a modern industrial place, but visitors come for the cheap leather goods in Avinguda General Luque and Gran Via de Colon. Thursday, market day, is Inca's busiest time, trading in souvenirs, household goods, flowers and food. Inca is also known for its traditional cuisine, including *caracoles* (snails), and its wine cellars converted into restaurants. ✪ *Map E3*

4 Sa Pobla

Perhaps the most impressive thing about this agricultural town is its cemetery, which has unusually beautiful monuments. The main square and mansion of Can Planes, which houses the Museu de la Jugueta *(see p68)*, are also attractive, and the town is noted for its Sunday market and January festival *(see p52)*. Otherwise, the place is fairly low key. ✪ *Map E2*

5 Muro

A pleasant, sleepy town full of old mansions and dominated by the church of Sant Joan Baptista. The adjacent belfry has wonderful views *(see p57)*. The Museu Etnológic *(see p63)* houses furniture, costumes, tools and instruments. ✪ *Map E3*

Left **Inca main square** Right **Altar of Sant Joan Baptista, Muro**

If you are buying wine at Binissalem, remember crianza is good, reserva even better and gran reserva the best

Petra

Petra

6 This small town is the birth-place of Junipero Serra. Aged 54, the pioneering Franciscan monk travelled to America and Mexico and after many arduous journeys on foot, founded missions in California. The old houses lining the labyrinth of narrow alleys have changed little since Serra's time here. The town makes the most of its famous son, and all places associated with Serra are well marked. These include a humble building in Carrer Barracar Alt where Serra was born. Next to this is a small museum, opened in 1955, devoted to his life and work, which includes wooden models of the nine American

Manacor's church

Mallorca's Windmills

Mallorca is famous for its hundreds of windmills, especially in the region of Es Pla. These ingenious devices have been used in the Mediterranean since at least the 7th century. Now replaced by motorized pumps, most stone windmills have fallen into disrepair and decrepitude. However, in the zone between Palma, Algaida and Llucmajor, ecology-minded farmers have installed modern metal windmills.

missions established by Serra. At the end of the street in which the Serra family house stands is the 17th-century monastery of Sant Bernat. A series of Majolica panels down a side street next to the monastery are a gift from grateful Californians and pay tribute to the monk. ✎ *Map F4*

Manacor

7 Mallorca's second city is famous for artificial pearl factories, of which Perlas Majórica *(see p124)* is the best-known, producing 50 million a year. The method, involving fish scales, repeated baking and polishing, can be witnessed on the free tour. Also look inside the Església de Nostra Senyora dels Dolors to find a figure of Christ with scraggly hair and a skirt, and pilgrims lining up to kiss his bloodstained feet. ✎ *Map F4*

For more on the isolated monasteries of Es Pla **see pp60–61**

8 Els Calderers

This country house chronicles 200 years of the life of Mallorca's gentry in a more modest version of Sa Granja (see pp16–17). Demonstrations of traditional methods are part of the tour, and you can see historic breeds of Mallorcan farm animals. ✪ Follow signs from MA-15 • Map E4 • 10am–5pm daily • Adm

9 Montuïri

Built on a hill, the town of Montuïri is famous for its agricultural produce. Nineteen of the original 24 windmills still stand as testimony to the town's former glory, striking in the landscape. The Ermita de Sant Miquel (see p61) is nearby, offering good views. ✪ Map E4

10 Gordiola Glassworks

The glassworks were founded in 1719, but the present castle-like, Neo-Gothic building dates from the 1960s. The place offers a unique opportunity to watch glass-blowers at work, and its world-class museum of glass (see p63) also fires enthusiasm for the substance. You can buy everything from cheap bibelots to chandeliers fit for a castle. ✪ Ctra. Palma-Manacor, Km 19, Algaida • Map D4 • 971 665046 • 9am–7pm Mon–Sat, 9am–1:30pm Sun • www.gordiola.com • Free

Els Calderers

A Day's Drive Through Es Pla

Morning

⏱ Begin in the north, at **Sa Pobla** (see p121), where you should be sure to visit the cemetery and **Museu de la Jugueta** (see p68). Proceed south to **Muro** (p121) for a look at the handsome Sant Joan Baptista church, Muro's famous bull ring and the **Museu Etnològic** (p63).

Drive through pretty Santa Margalida, then Maria de la Salut, and on to medieval Sineu, at the geographic centre of the island, where you can stroll and have a drink at **Café Sa Plaça** café (see p124).

By now, it should be about lunchtime, so continue on to **Petra** to have a wonderfully elegant meal at **Sa Plaça** (see p125), and to check out the hometown of Fray Junípero Serra.

Afternoon

After lunch, make your way on through Sant Joan and then to appealing **Montuïri**, with its signature windmills. Next, cut down to Porreres and take the road from there to Llucmajor. Be sure to stop off along the way for a walk around the quaintly picturesque grounds of the Finca Son Sama.

The last leg of the journey is to head back north to Algaida, being sure to pop into Raïms for a look at its timeless charm.

Finally, just to the west of Algaida, take a prolonged tour of the **Gordiola Glassworks**, with its superb museum and shop.

Left **Wines, Binissalem** Right **Camper shoe factory sign**

TOP 10 Cafés and Shops

1 Café Sa Plaça, Sineu
A pleasant café in the square, where you can study the magnificent church of Santa María and listen to the birds chirping *(see p81).* ◈ *Sa Plaça, 17 • 971 520664*

2 Bar Ca'n Tomeu, Petra
By the main square, this bar has a local feel and decor. You'll find *pa amb oli (see p78),* tapas and salads. ◈ *C/Sol, 47 • 971 561023*

3 Tejidos Artesania, Santa Maria del Camí
The only manufacturer of *robes de llengües* (tongue of flame cloth) that still uses traditional methods on antique looms. Tablecloths and other furnishings are sold *(see p70).* ◈ *Artesania Textil Bujosa, C/ Bernardo Santa Eugenia, 53 (E of Bunyola) • 971 620054 • www.bujosatextil.com*

4 José L. Ferrer, Binissalem
The famous winery is worth a stop for both the tour and the wine-tasting. You'll find the reds, made from Mantonegro and Callet grapes, and the white, made from Moll. ◈ *C/Conquistador, 103 • 971 511050 • www.vinosferrer.com • Wine tasting at 11am & 4:30pm Mon–Fri • Adm*

5 Camper Factory Outlet, Inca
The famous Spanish shoes are made right here and you can have first pick of the newest styles at reduced prices. Follow the billboards featuring a huge foot. ◈ *Poligono Industrial, off main road • 971 888361 • www.camper.es*

6 Antony's Conexion, Inca
This huge shop sells all kinds of leather goods from the best labels in Spain, as well as from its own Conexion brand. The Antony's Market section features the day's best bargains. ◈ *C/Sineu, s/n • 971 504266 • www.antonysconexion.com*

7 Kollflex, Selva
The well-known brand has been producing excellent jackets, accessories and shoes for shops all over the world since 1927. You can take a brief factory tour and browse through the large shop. ◈ *Carretera de Lluc, 45 (north of Inca) • 971 515027 • www.kollflex.com*

8 Perlas Majorica, Manacor
Tour the best-known factory *(see p122),* where the sight of imperfect pearls being smashed can be unnerving. Then enter the large showroom, usually thronged with avid buyers. The glass-cored gems come in every colour and setting imaginable. ◈ *Palma-Artá road, km 47 • 971 550900 • 9am–7pm Mon–Fri; 9am–1pm Sat & Sun • Free*

9 Art-Metall, Manacor
The place to find the wrought-iron objects seen all over the island – candelabra, mirrors etc. ◈ *C/Cid Campeador, 2 • 971 555922*

10 Gordiola Glassworks, Baixos
A great collection of glass from around the world, from ancient to modern, and an amazing array of glass merchandise *(see p123).*

Recommend your favourite café on traveldk.com

Price Categories
For a three-course meal for one with half a bottle of wine (or equivalent meal), taxes and extra charges.

€ under €20
€€ €20–€30
€€€ €30–€40
€€€€ €40–€50
€€€€€ over €50

Left **Read's Hotel** Right **Leon de Sineu**

TOP 10 Places to Eat

1 Bacchus, Read's Hotel, Santa Maria del Camí
The dining room of this Michelin star restaurant is defined by two arches, Classical frescoes and of a balustrade overlooking the sea. The food is close to perfect *(see p83)*. ✆ 971 140261 • www.readshotel. com • Closed lunch Mon–Fri • €€€€€

2 Molí des Torrent, Santa Maria del Camí
Set in a restored windmill, Molí des Torrent serves traditional Mallorcan dishes with a German twist. There is a good wine list and an excellent range of German beers. ✆ Ctra. de Bunyola, 75 • 971 140503 • www.molidestorrent.de • Closed Wed, Thu • €€€€

3 Celler C'An Amer, Inca
A traditional wine cellar serving sturdy portions of typical Mallorcan dishes accompanied by a good range of local wines. ✆ C/Pau, 39 • 971 501261 • €€€

4 Leon de Sineu, Sineu
Light, international cuisine is served in the garden or inside under a broad Catalan arch. Octopus salad, meatballs stuffed with squid and other delicious Mediterranean dishes have flair. ✆ C/dels Bous, 129 • 971 520211 • No dis acc • €€€

5 Celler Es Grop, Sineu
The restaurant is housed in an atmospheric wine bodega. Choose from *lechona* (suckling pig), *arroz brut* (peasant rice),

tumbet (stewed vegetables) and *caracoles* (snails). ✆ C/Major, 18 • 971 520187 • No dis acc • Closed Mon • €€

6 Sa Plaça, Petra
The freshest food is served in a charming setting of flowers, antiques and classical music. The chicken liver pâté and courgettes (zucchini) stuffed with salmon are incredible. ✆ Plaça Ramon Llull, 4 • 971 561646 • Closed Tue • €€€

7 Es Molí d'en Perons, Montuïri
Es Molí serves creative dishes such as giltfish in Cava sauce or duck with apricot and sesame. Fine views over the Mallorcan plain. ✆ C/Es Molinar, 51 • 971 646508 • €€€

8 Es Mirador, Ctra. Llucmajor-Porreres
Try mushrooms, snails or brochettes of rabbit, lamb or quail. The place has an ancient, rustic feel *(see also p143)*. ✆ Km 3.5 • 971 120959 • Closed Sun • €€

9 Es Recó de Randa, Algaida
A tranquil place with inventive cuisine, including aubergine (eggplant) stuffed with salt cod. The tasting menu is excellent. ✆ C/ Font, 21, Randa • 971 660997 • €€€€

10 C'an Mateu, Algaida
Set in a 400-year-old inn, the restaurant is popular with locals, and local meats and vegetables are used for traditional dishes, such as snails in broth. ✆ Ctra. Vieja de Manacor, km 21 • 971 665036 • €€€

Note: Unless otherwise stated, all restaurants have disabled access, accept credit cards and serve vegetarian meals

STREETSMART

STREETSMART

Left **Internet sign** Centre **Tourist information sign** Right **Airport sign**

TOP 10 Planning Your Trip

Climate
1 Mallorca has mild, humid winters, and hot, dry summers. Expect daytime temperatures in winter to be above 12°C (53°F), and in summer not to fall below 30°C (86°F).

When to Go
2 Summer is high season in Mallorca. Autumn is thus a better time to visit, when the weather is still great, the water at its warmest and prices lower. Hiking and cycling are best in April. Nature lovers should come in spring or autumn, when birds are on the move and wildflowers are blooming.

Visas and Red Tape
3 EU citizens can enter Spain with just their valid ID card. Britons, Americans, Australians, New Zealanders and Canadians need only a valid passport for automatic permission to stay 90 days. Other nationalities should check with their consulate. Most hotels will request your ID card or passport.

Spanish Embassies and Consulates
4 Spanish embassies or consulates in your home country can provide information about visiting, studying, working and retiring in Spain.

Spanish National Tourist Offices
5 This service will load you up with maps, pamphlets and brochures upon request. Contact them in your home country or, better still, pay them a visit if possible.

Mallorcan Tourist Offices
6 The tourist offices in Palma and across Mallorca are staffed by multilingual people who have a good knowledge of the island.

Internet Information
7 Mallorcans are not heavy users of the Internet, but there are some good multilingual web guides, as listed in the Directory.

Languages
8 The local language is Mallorquí, a dialect of Catalan, but Castilian (Spanish) is also spoken everywhere. Signs can be a confusing mixture of both. Many islanders who work in the tourist industry can also speak German and English, and often French, Italian and more.

Insurance
9 It is a good idea to take out private medical insurance, even if your country has reciprocal medical arrangements with Spain. Then, should you require treatment while on holiday, you will simply pay for the care, keep the receipts, and be reimbursed according to the terms of your policy. General travel insurance to cover flight cancellation and theft is also strongly recommended.

What to Take
10 Casual dress is generally acceptable, so bring lightweight, loose-fitting linens or cottons. A hat may also be useful, and don't forget your favourite sunscreen and other pharmaceutical items. At least one dressy outfit is a good idea if you plan to visit an upmarket restaurant or club.

Directory

Spanish Embassies and Consulates
• *UK (020) 7589 8989*
• *USA (212) 355 4080*
• *Canada (613) 747 2252*
• *Australia (02) 6273 3555*

Mallorcan Tourist Board
Plaça de la Reina, 2, Palma de Mallorca; 971 173990

Spanish National Tourist Offices
• *UK: 79 New Cavendish St, London; (0870) 850 6599* • *USA: 666 5th Ave, New York; (212) 265 8822* • *Canada: 2 Bloor St West, Toronto; (416) 916 3131* • *Singapore: 541 Orchard Rd, #09-04 Liat Towers, Singapore; (65) 737 3008*

Internet Information
• *www.illesbalears.es*
• *www.spain.info*
• *www.mallorcaonline. com*
• *www.newsmallorca. com*

Previous pages **Forn des Teatre pastry shop, Palma**

Left **Palma airport** Centre **Cruise ship** Right **Typical hairpin bend on the island**

🔟 Getting to Mallorca

1 By Air from the Mainland

Scheduled flights and charters connect with all major Spanish and European cities. Visitors from the US will have to make the connection somewhere in Europe. Mallorca's airport is located 11 km (6 miles) southeast of Palma, with taxis and buses transporting visitors to the city and resorts.

2 By Air from Ibiza and Menorca

There are daily flights from Ibiza and Menorca to Palma with Air Nostrum (part of Iberia) and other carriers. Last-minute places are available, but book ahead in high season.

3 Charters

Cheap charter flights are readily available (as are flights from the "no frills" airlines), but dates and times are fixed, and any refund unlikely. Spanair fly from Spanish cities – their one-way tickets are fairly priced.

4 Packages

Many travel agents offer packages including full- or half-board lodgings as well as flight and transfers, usually to the crowded, mass-market resorts.

5 By Ferry from the Mainland

Ferries and jetfoils run from Barcelona and Valencia (via Ibiza). The best bet is Trasmediterránea's jetfoil (a catamaran that in season does the trip twice a day in 3–4 hours (the other ferries will take up to 10 hours). The ride is generally comfortable and offers great previews of the mountainous western coast as you circle around the island to berth at the port of Palma. Buying a return ticket saves money.

6 By Ferry from Ibiza and Menorca

Trasmediterránea runs a regular ferry service from Ibiza and Menorca to Palma. Baleària runs a Dénia–Ibiza–Palma service with no stop in Menorca. Cape Balear de Cruceros offers a passenger-only service to and from Cala Rajada, while Iscomar serves Port d'Alcúdia.

7 Bringing a Car

Fast ferries can be taken from Barcelona and Valencia. Inter-island ferries also carry cars, but some must be booked in advance in summer. (Hire cars cannot be transferred between islands.)

8 Cruises

Many cruise ships stop at Mallorca as part of a typical 10- or 15-day tour of Mediterranean ports. Cruise passengers rarely have enough time for any more than Palma's top sights and shops.

9 Private Boat

Marinas are dotted around the Mallorcan coastline, with no spot more desirable than Port Portals near Portals Nous *(see p44)*, where members of the Spanish royal family usually moor their yachts. Port d'Andratx *(see p40)* is also well thought of, but there are many cheaper options.

10 Private Plane

Except for the odd private landing strip, all planes have to land at Palma airport. Balloon trips are an entertaining option on the east coast *(see directory)*.

Directory

Palma Airport
902 404704

Airlines
• British Airways 0844 493 0787; www. britishairways.com
• Air Europa: 902 401 501; www.aireuropa. com • Iberia 902 400500 • Spanair: National 902 131415; www.spanair.com
• easyJet: 0871 244 2366 www.easyjet.com

Ferries
• Trasmediterránea 902 454645 www. trasmediterranea.es
• Baleària 902 160180 www.balearia.com
• Iscomar 902 119128 www.iscomar.com
• Private Cruises 679 906919 www. crucerosmansaya.com

Mallorca Balloons
971 818182; www. mallorcaballoons.com

Left **Horse and cart for tourists, Palma** Centre **Parking meter sign** Right **Cyclists, Platja de Palma**

Getting Around Mallorca

1 Buses
Mallorca has an extensive network of buses. The central station is at Plaça Espanya in Palma; get a general timetable from any tourist agency. Palma also has a good urban bus system (EMT). Buy tickets on board.

2 Trains and Trams
There are two railway lines on the island: one from Palma to Sóller, the other Palma to Inca, Sa Pobla and Manacor. They have separate stations in Palma's Plaça Espanya. The delightful Sóller train offers special tourist trips in the morning, for an extra cost, between April and October. The more utilitarian Inca train stops everywhere. An attractive tram runs from Sóller to Port de Sóller *(see p68)*.

3 Driving
Driving here can be fun, so long as you're in no hurry. The Palma–Sóller and Palma–Inca roads are the only major highways. Other roads, though narrow and twisting, are in good repair for the most part, though you will need nerves of steel in some areas *(see p132)*. Driving is the only way to see some of the sights and to fit a lot into one trip *(see pp48–9)*.

4 Motorbikes
This is a popular option as most of the Mallorcan roads are ideally suited for scooting around on a two-wheeler. Motorbikes and scooters can be rented in most towns.

5 Hiring a Vehicle
Car hire is quite cheap. Most big agencies are represented at Palma airport, or you can contact some directly to make comparisons. You'll need to be 21 or over, with a driver's licence and a credit card. Smaller cars are better for the narrow lanes.

6 Boats
Taking a boat is the only way to see some of Mallorca's most beautiful coves and cliffs that are inaccessible by road.

7 Taxis
Getting around by taxi – at least within the city of Palma – is quite a reasonable proposition. Fares are moderate, and there are enough taxis in circulation to give you a good chance of flagging one down at any time of day or night. A taxi ride across the whole island will cost from €90.

8 Cycling
Cycling along country lanes and mountain roads is an excellent mode of

Sóller tram

transport. Tandems and all sorts of other pedalling options are available for hire *(see p46)*.

9 Gentle Walks
Some of the bigger port towns offer lovely promenades right along the water's edge. One of the best is the pedestrian-only Passeig Anglada Camarassa–Voramar in Port de Pollença. Port de Sóller also has a broad path that loops around much of its beautiful bay.

10 Long-Distance Walks
Much of Mallorca is rough territory and perfect for hiking. Easy slopes with lots of vegetation can be found all over the island, but if you want real challenges, there are several rugged mountain trails, many of which are signposted from town to town *(see pp46 & 48–9)*.

Directory

http://tib.caib.es (for all public transport info)

Buses
• 971 177777

Trains
• 902 364711

Taxis in Palma
• 971 401414
• 971 755440
• 971 728081

Car Hire
• Avis 902 110261
• Europcar 902 105030
• Hertz 971 789670

The normal abbreviations for roads are: "C/" for Carrer (Street), "Avda." for Avinguda (Avenue) and "Ctra." for Carretera (Highway)

Left **Pharmacy, Palma** Centre **Health shop sign, Andratx** Right **Hospital, Palma**

ᴛᴏᴘ10 Health and Security

1 Emergency Numbers

You can dial the free number 112 in any type of emergency; they speak English and will alert the appropriate service. There are also free direct numbers for the fire brigade, ambulance service, national police, Guárdia Civil or the local police (see box). Be ready to give precise information about what is needed and where you are.

2 Accidents

An alternative source of help if you have an accident of any sort is the Creu Roja (Red Cross), who will send an ambulance and paramedics.

3 Health Issues

No inoculations are required or advised prior to your visit. Sunburn and heatstroke are the main sources of discomfort for visitors – use sunscreen, wear a hat and drink plenty of bottled water. Some people experience a minor stomach upset, which is more likely to be from exposure to different bacteria in the food and water than real food poisoning (see p132).

4 Prescriptions

Bring any prescription medicines you might require, packed in your carry-on bag, not checked luggage. This is because Spanish pharmaceuticals may differ from those in your home country in name, dosage and form.

5 Farmacias

Pharmacists are well trained and a good source of advice for minor complaints. Some speak very good English and might be able to sell you medicines that would normally be available only by prescription in your home country. In Palma, many pharmacies (farmacias) are open 24 hours.

6 Multilingual Doctors

If you are seriously ill and need a doctor who speaks your language, ask your local consulate, hotel, pharmacy or tourist office for contacts. If you need someone who works under the EU health plan, make sure that the doctor is part of the Spanish healthcare system; otherwise, be prepared to pay on the spot and be reimbursed later by your insurance company.

7 Medical Treatment

To claim back medical costs, EU citizens should obtain a European Health Insurance Card prior to travelling. Not everything is covered by the card, so additional health insurance is advised.

8 Disabled Travellers

Mallorca is not well equipped for disabled visitors. However, the law requires that all new public buildings have disabled access – the newest hotels are your best bet (see p135).

9 Petty Crime

In any crowded area, there are bound to be pickpockets about. Often working in pairs, they create distractions – sometimes very elaborate ploys – then fleece the unwary. The best solution is not to carry valuables in purses, bum bags or outside pockets, and not to leave your bags unattended for an instant.

10 Serious Crime

Long gone are the centuries when Mallorca was rife with rampaging brigands and banditos. Serious crime is virtually unheard of on this pleasure-loving isle. However, avoid wandering through deserted, unlit alleys at night, especially in the seedier parts of Palma, which – as anywhere in the world – are the territory of muggers.

Directory

Emergency Numbers
- Any emergency 112
- Fire 080
- Ambulance 061
- National Police 091
- Civil Guard 062
- Local Police 092

Creu Roja (Red Cross)
- 902 222292

International Hospitals in Palma
- Policlínica Miramar 971 767000 www. policlinicamiramar.com
- Clínica Juaneda 971 731647 www.clinica juaneda.es

Left **Street trading** Right **"Grand Prix" track, Península de Formentor**

TOP 10 Things to Avoid

1 Tap Water
Water is a problem on the island, which, having no rivers at all and entire seasons without any rain, suffers from quasi-drought conditions most of the time. You'll see huge tank trucks transporting drinking water all around the island, but in general it's better to drink only bottled water, since much of the potable water sits in cisterns for quite a long time.

2 Rancid Food
In the heat of summer, check the freshness of what you consume. Tapas dishes that look as if they have been around a day too long, anything with mayonnaise that's been sitting out of the fridge, and shellfish served in less than fastidiously hygienic establishments – all are probably best refused.

3 Bad Manners
Dress respectfully when you visit Mallorca's churches, and don't visit at all during services unless you genuinely want to join in. Nudism is legal on all beaches but check with hotel staff as to which are the ones where this practice is more common.

4 Fakes and Forgeries
In the land of Miró, Dalí, Picasso and other greats, it's wise to be wary of supposed "originals" by any of these masters.

Copies, prints, forgeries and outright fakes do a brisk business. To avoid them, check your dealer's credentials and ask for certificates of authentication and guarantees.

5 "Mystery" Tours
Especially in the heavily touristed zones, you might be offered a tour that, on the face of it, looks like something for nothing. It might be a daytrip to an interesting sight at a cut-rate price, or an offer of cash or a lavish meal just for going to inspect a new condo project. These are not promotional bargains in the usual sense, but hard sales ploys that should be avoided.

6 Beach Snacks
Most of the snack bars you find along the popular beaches are overpriced and low quality, with a few exceptions. Just use them for a drink and simple snack, such as a *pa amb oli*. For real meals, head to our recommended eateries.

7 Flower Girls
These gypsy women appear friendly enough when they hand you a flower or a sprig of "lucky" rosemary. If you accept, however, they suddenly transform into indignant creatures demanding a lot of money for their cheery "gift". Do your best to dodge them and their little scam.

8 Peddlers
Most pavement peddlers will do little more than call out a word or two about their merchandise. But as soon as you show an interest, you may be in for a lot of pressure to buy. Make it clear that you'll decide what, if anything, you're going to buy. Check all merchandise, especially clothing, for defects, then offer half of the asking price.

9 Trileros
You'll see this ageold gambling trick in busy pedestrian areas. The main man shuffles three cups, showing you how easy it is to follow the one that covers the hidden object. Usually, there is an accomplice among the onlookers who makes it appear very easy to win. The con is exposed when gullible tourists try their luck and quickly begin losing.

10 Hair-Raising Roads
If Grand Prix-style driving is not to your liking, it's best to keep driving to a minimum along Mallorca's most challenging mountain roads – especially if any of your passengers suffers from carsickness or panic attacks. Though most roads are wellmaintained, they can be exceedingly narrow, subject to hairpin bends around yawning chasms. The state of roads is noted throughout this book.

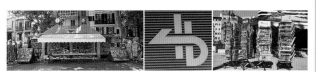

Left **Kiosk** Centre **Bank logo** Right **Racks of newspapers**

🔟 Banking and Communications

1 Exchange
Since the euro became the currency of Spain and many other realms, life is much easier for most visitors. Admittedly, the changeover from pesetas to euros resulted in some price inflation, but, for the most part, it's easier to tell how much you're spending.

2 Traveller's Cheques
Traveller's cheques are a useful safety precaution but they are rarely accepted in hotels or shops and changing them will incur a commission fee.

3 ATMs
For proper cash, ATMs are the very best option: readily available and reliable. Spanish banks do not charge transaction fees, though your own bank is likely to charge a fee for using a non-branch machine. A good procedure is to get the maximum each time (usually €300), in which case the fee will probably be only about 4% on your money drawn out. But keep your cash hidden.

4 Credit Cards
Credit cards can be used for most transactions but could be a problem for some budget hotels, cheap restaurants, art galleries and small places in remote outposts. Be aware that your own bank may charge you a 2% conversion fee for every card purchase you make – a sum that can add up shockingly.

5 Wiring Money
Only as a last resort. You can have your bank send money to a bank on the island, but expect it to take an indeterminate number of days, and for high charges to be levied.

6 Mail
Post offices *(correus)* are open only in the morning, except for the main post office in Palma. You can also get stamps *(segells)* for letters and postcards at tobacco shops and newspaper stands. Spanish mail is usually reliable, but inevitably sometimes even priority mail fails to reach its destination.

7 Phones
Phones provided in hotel rooms are convenient but expensive. Most public phone booths accept credit cards, phonecards and coins, and can be used for local and international calls. Mobile phones work well almost everywhere, but check with your provider before leaving your home country.

8 Internet
Most hotels have Internet facilities, and there are many cafés and bars in the larger towns *(see p81)* that offer the service, as well as a few specific Internet points in Palma *(see p92)*.

9 Newspapers and Magazines
In hotels and kiosks in larger towns you'll find a good selection of the international editions of major North American and European newspapers and the English-language *Mallorca Daily Bulletin*, which is published every day except Monday. It publicises what's on and lists the island's markets.

🔟 TV and Radio
The upper-tier hotels all offer satellite TV, with many German channels and some in English, French or Italian. There are several German-language radio stations, and the BBC World Service is on FM 95.8. Stations in Spanish, Catalan and Mallorquí feature a broad mix of Spanish and international pop music.

Directory

General Post Office
C/de la Constitució, 6, Palma • 971 228610 • 8:30am–8:30pm Mon–Fri, 9:30am–2pm Sat

International Codes
• *Country code when dialling from abroad: +34*
• *Dialling abroad from Mallorca: 00, then country code, area code and local number*

Directory Enquiries
• *Local and national 11818*
• *International 11825*

Note: *while you're in Mallorca, you must always dial the area code, 971, even if just calling next door*

133

Left **Aquacity water-park** Centre **Toys Palace, Pollença** Right **Miniature truck, Platja de Palma**

Tips for Families

1 Visitor and Expat Demographics

Mallorca is exceptionally well geared to families and also has a number of thriving expat communities. The majority of visitors are German, as evidenced by the German-language signs, radio stations and satellite channels. Colònia de Sant Jordi is virtually a German enclave, while Portocolom has a greater concentration of Britons. Other corners of the island (such as Port de Pollença) have a thorough mix of nationalities.

2 Accommodation

Unless they specify "adults only", most places in Mallorca truly welcome families. Hotels often let you include any number of children up to a certain age – sometimes as old as the teens – at no extra charge, except perhaps a nominal fee for the extra bed or two. The best option for most families is a self-catering apartment.

3 Hotel Programmes

Larger hotels and resorts may have a programme of activities for guests of every age. These may run from water aerobics, water polo or other exercise regimes, to crafts classes for adults and organized games for pre-schoolers. Most such activities are scheduled on a weekly basis, with a monthly calendar posted

in some conspicuous spot in the hotel lobby.

4 Babysitting

Many hotels offer babysitting services, especially those that cater primarily or exclusively to package tourists. The cost of the service is usually included in the package. There may also be a supervised play area for kids aged 4–8 or so.

5 Family Meals

Most restaurants are happy to cater for children. Some offer a separate menu to please a child's palate, and many will prepare special foods for infants, so that you don't have to depend on commercial brands all the time.

6 Merchandise for Children

There are shops galore focusing on kids' needs and wants – toys, beach gear, clothes and gadgets. International brands of nappies and babyfood are widely available. Most of the merchandise is cheap enough for you not to fret about leaving it behind in preference to lugging it back home.

7 Fun Cultural and Ecological Sights

Many of Mallorca's theme parks and museums have exhibits and activities designed entirely with children in mind. Nature parks are of interest to many children, and Mallorca's caves are very

likely to be a big hit with your youngsters (see pp68–9).

8 Beaches and Water-parks

Besides the obvious family attractions of building sandcastles and splashing around in the sea, Mallorca also has some great commercial water-parks. The whole family can participate at these, with your children burning up a full-day's worth of energy. Outdoor zoos and aquariums are incorporated into some (see pp68–9).

9 Attractions for Your Teenagers

In addition to the family-oriented theme parks, there's plenty of high-energy action for your teenage children, such as windsurfing, snorkelling, boating and hiking (see pp46–9).

10 Nightlife

In terms of nightlife, you will have to exercise parental judgement about any ground rules and curfews for teenage children in your party. Obviously, some of the brasher resorts are the domain of older teenagers and young adults who travel in groups without families, seeking only the beach and nightlife. Some of the nightclubs cater mainly to the younger crowd, while others have a more diverse mix of ages (see pp72–3).

Give your children sunhats, plaster them with a high-factor sunscreen and limit their time in the sun

Left **Wheelchair priority sign** Centre **Airport taxi** Right **Beach visitor information**

TOP 10 Tips for Disabled Travellers

1 Access at the Airport
Historically lagging in providing for people with mobility problems, Mallorca has finally begun to catch up in recent years. At Palma airport you can find adequate facilities if you have a disablity – as long as you notify your travel agent and/or your airline of your needs well in advance, and then reconfirm a week or so before departure.

2 Hotel Access
The older hotels – often refurbished medieval structures – rarely have facilities for the disabled. The best bet is to book into the newest hotel you can find, where elevators should be big enough and bathroom sizes etc will comply with EU laws. But double-check the details before booking.

3 Wheelchair-Friendly Buses
All buses in Palma are now able to handle wheelchair-bound travellers, including those going to and from the airport. Contact the municipal transport authority, EMT, for more information.

4 Cars and Taxis
Specially-equipped vehicles are rare, but taxi drivers do their best to help disabled passengers. Mallorca Taxis (www. mallorcataxi.com) have cars adapted for wheelchairs, called Eurotaxis.

5 Trains
Mallorca's trains are old and in no way accommodating to independent wheelchair users. The only way to use them is to board with assistance and stow your wheelchair for the duration of the journey.

6 Restaurants
Many restaurants present the problems of lots of steps and levels. Then again, staff are usually very willing to help, so you can generally manage to dine at any restaurant of your choice.

7 Public Buildings
Public buildings in Palma and other cities are being brought up to speed with EU regulations on accessibility. Many museums, for example, are being completely remodelled to allow for ramps and large elevators. Still, there are just as many sights that, due to their age and decrepitude, remain off-limits to those with limited mobility.

8 Public Conveniences
Again, in museums and other public buildings, toilet facilities are being remodelled to allow for wheelchair access. But most other public toilets have tiny cubicles.

9 Resources in Spain
The Spanish National Tourist Office (see p128) can give you the latest news on disabled facilities. The national organization for the visually impaired, ONCE, can provide Braille maps and arrange aspects of your trip through its travel agency, Viajes 2000.

10 Other Resources
Several good good English-language websites promote independent travel by providing information, practical tips and encouragement. Some will even help you plan the details of your trip.

Directory

Wheelchair-Friendly Buses
• EMT: 971 431024

Resources in Spain
• Viajes 2000: C/Foners, 7, Palma; 971 774684; www.viajes2000.com

Other Resources
• Access-Able Travel Services: www.access-able.com
• Sath (USA): 212-447-7284, www.sath.org
• Accessible Travel (UK): (01452) 729739; www.accessibletravel.co.uk
• Mobility International USA, Eugene, OR, (541) 343-1284; www.miusa.org
• National Disability Services (NDS) (Australia): (02) 6283 32 00; www.nds.org.au

Left **Café sign, Port d'Alcúdia** Centre **Pub sign, Portocolom** Right **Daily lunch menu**

Budget Tips

1 Off-Season Bargains
Coming out of season is by far the best way to make your holiday money go further in Mallorca. Prices plummet as the throngs of July and August become only a faint memory in the minds of hoteliers and restaurateurs. Low-season prices for everything can delight the budget-minded traveller, plus you have the luxury of being one of only a few, rather than one of uncountable thousands.

2 Package Deals
If you choose the location carefully, an all-inclusive package can mean excellent value. Make sure that transfers, taxes and other extras are also covered.

3 Self-Catering
If you can book far in advance, you should be able to secure one of the cheaper self-catering apartments in a pretty seaside town with good facilities (see p147). Rural tourism is becoming increasingly popular and renting a country home (casa rural) or apartment can be surprisingly inexpensive.

4 Camping
There are no official camp sites in Mallorca and camping rough is prohibited in urban areas and in zones prohibited for military or other reasons. You are allowed to camp rough elsewhere, but try to obtain permission from the landowner first.

5 Picnicking
Given the wealth of natural beauty on the island, much of it now given over to reserves, picnicking is a great proposal generally. There are also plenty of grocery stores out of which you can construct a memorable pastoral repast on the cheap.

6 Partying on a Budget
Not all pubs and clubs are pricey. Some of the best, in fact, do not impose a cover charge or minimum fee. And most pubs are so busy that no one will notice you nursing your brew all night.

7 IVA Sales Tax
Non-EU residents can reclaim IVA (VAT) on single items worth over €90 bought in shops with a "Tax-free shopping" sign, within 6 months of purchase. Pay the full price and ask for a tax-free cheque, which must be stamped when you leave Spain. The refund can be made on your credit card.

8 Make Lunch the Main Meal
The daily lunch menu in most restaurants can save you a lot of money – as much as 75% of the à la carte cost (see menú del dia, opposite). Portions are often generous, too, so you can make this your major meal of the day. It's also a great way to savour the cuisine of some of the top restaurants without forking out their top prices.

9 Laundromats
Unfortunately, regular laundries and tintorenás (dry-cleaners) are quite expensive, and hotel services even more exorbitant. However, some hotels offer clients the use of their washers for a nominal fee. A few lavanderías automáticas can be found in Palma, but don't bother looking anywhere else.

10 Reduced Admissions
Coupons for reduced group admissions to various attractions can help a lot when you've got a whole family to pay for. You'll find them in magazines, weekly papers, fliers and brochures. They are also handed out on the street, and tourist offices often have stacks of them.

Directory

Package deals
• www.expedia.co.uk
• www.thefirst resort.com
• www.bargain holidays.com

Self Catering
• www.toprural.com
• www.selfcatering hols.com

Left **Breakfast** Centre **Café sign** Right **Evening meal at a restaurant in Palma**

🔟 Drinking and Eating Tips

1 Eating Out
Both lunch and dinner hours tend to be late. Lunchtime is certainly no earlier than 1:30pm, and even 2:30pm is perfectly normal. Dinnertime can be no earlier than 8:30pm, and sitting down at 11pm is not unheard of. A reservation is never a bad idea, but don't worry about dressing up.

2 Breakfast
Throughout most of the Mediterranean, breakfast is little more than a wolfed-down coffee and *pasta* (pastry). As a visitor, however, you are free to linger and add other foods to the meal. Foreign-run venues may offer a full English or American breakfast, and many hotels cater to international taste with a full buffet.

3 Tapas and Racions
Tapas are a Spanish institution. What began in ages past as a free slice of ham laid across a drink has turned into small portions of anything you can think of, some of it very creative. Locals eat them as appetizers before heading off to dinner, but a few well-chosen tapas can easily make a full meal *(see p79)*. Racions are normal-sized portions for sharing.

4 Menú del Dia
Many places offer a *menú del dia* (daily menu) at lunchtime, which is usually cheaper than à la carte prices. You get a limited choice of a first course (typically soup or salad) and second course (fish or meat, with sides) and dessert, with water and wine included. Coffee is usually extra, or offered in place of dessert.

5 Meats
Pork in all its guises is the central meat in the Mallorcan diet, with roast suckling pig considered the crowning glory. Duck, rabbit, quail and other game are more common than beef and veal. Goat and lamb feature on many Mallorcan menus.

6 Seafood
The waters around the island were fished out long ago, so fishermen go further afield to haul in the Mediterranean bounty. A local favourite is *rape* (monkfish), as well as lobsters, crayfish, prawns and mussels.

7 Side Dishes and Desserts
Favourite side dishes include asparagus, both green and white, and mushrooms sautéed with garlic, as well as whatever vegetables may be at their seasonal best. Fresh fruit is always an option for dessert, along with almond cake and almond ice cream, but one of the most characteristic is *crema catalana*, a kind of crème bruleé or custard with a crispy, caramelized sugar topping.

8 Drinks
Wine and beer are the top choices, usually accompanied by a small bottle of mineral water, either still or sparkling. Note that the sparkling is very fizzy indeed and tends to be salty. Sangria is prevalent on the island, and Cava (sparkling white wine) is delicious and inexpensive. A good aperitif choice is *fino* or *manzanilla* (sherry), or a host of mixed drinks, often involving local white rum or gin. Finally, coffee can be either *café sol* (espresso) or *cortado* ("cut" with either cold or hot milk). Ask for it *descafeinat* if you don't want the jolt.

9 Vegetarian and Vegan Options
Tumbet, a local vegetable stew, features on many traditional menus, but even the vegetable soups are usually enhanced with a bit of pork. One good recourse would be to have the chef compose a salad for you, leaving out the non-vegetarian ingredients. Or head for one of the fine vegetarian restaurants *(see p93)*.

10 Tipping
Tipping is not the absolute necessity here that it is in some countries. Nevertheless, it is customary to leave about 10% of the total bill, or at least to round the figure up – assuming you found the service satisfactory.

 If squiggly squid and other local favourites are not to your liking, you'll find sufficient international eateries to turn to

Left **Ceramics shop, Sóller** Right **Deli, Palma** Right **Spicy peppers and melons for sale**

🔟 Shopping Tips

1 Factory Outlets
Several of these bargain-hunters' dreams are sprinkled around the island, mostly in the Central Plain. Prominent on the list are Inca for leather goods, Santa Maria del Camí for traditional textiles and Manacor for artificial pearls *(see p124 for all of the above)*. Gordiola, near Algaida, is good for glassware *(see p123)*.

2 Markets
Traditional markets abound on Mallorca. Every day of the week, you'll find at least a couple of them going on some-where. In Palma, there's also a flea market, Rastrillo, every Saturday morning, 8am–2pm, on Avenida Gabriel Alomar i Villalonga. For Mallorca's best markets, *see p71*.

3 Haggling
Bargaining, especially if you buy more than one of something, is perfectly acceptable if you are buying in local markets. In fact, most market stall holders will automatically round your final bill down without your even asking for a deal. So feel free to practise your negotiating skills to the fullest.

4 Sales Tax
An 18% IVA is auto-matically included in the price of most goods, and 8% on services, but establish in advance if it is included when you are

buying a more expensive item, as it may make quite a difference.

5 Hours and Holidays
In general, shops and other public institutions keep old-fashioned Medi-terranean hours: they close for several hours for lunch and a siesta. Expect most places to be open 9am–1:30pm, 4–7pm Monday to Friday, though there will be plenty of variation, such as closing at 2pm and opening up again at 5pm for three hours. On Saturdays, most smaller shops are open morning only. Chain stores, tourist places and department stores will stay open all day and late into the evening. Public and religious holidays occur throughout the year and number about 15.

6 Sales
Price reductions are commonplace throughout the year, the biggest being in January and July. End-of-season sales are indicated by *"rebaixes"* signs in shop windows.

7 Crafts
Olive-wood carving, lace-making, embroidery, weaving, basketry, pottery and glass-blowing are all going strong on the island. There are many direct out-lets and stores that carry a range of crafts; the best of them are represented in the *Around the Island* listings in this guide.

8 Peddlers
Inevitably, you'll see blankets laid out on the pavements with all sorts of merchandise: clothing, African sculpture, hippie accessories ... whatever sells. Each town has its own area where such entrepreneurs display their wares, much of it at ridiculously low prices compared to the shops. But caveat emptor – check the goods carefully and look out for signs of shoddiness! All may not be what it first appears.

9 Foreign Books
Palma has several bookshops that carry literature of all sorts in foreign languages – we've listed one that specializes in secondhand books and has loads of great holiday reads *(see p91)*. Travel books about Mallorca in all languages are readily available just about everywhere, and booklets about specific sights are usually for sale in gifts shops.

10 Shipping and Customs
Most reputable shops will gladly see to shipping your purchases home – for a fee, of course. But you can do it yourself via the Spanish postal service or an international courier such as DHL or UPS. You will have to check if the merchandise you intend sending back incurs import duty in your home country.

Left **Pollença hotels** Right **Bendinat resort hotels**

🔟 Accommodation Tips

1 Area Options
This really rather small island offers a tremendous range of climes and terrains, from sophisticated city life to nearly alpine mountains, and from lush subtropical beaches to remote and wild plains. If you have the time, sample the diversity.

2 Determining Needs
Its worth thinking about what you require of your accommodation. A conventional hotel room with private bath and balcony, possibly with meals included in the price? Or would a self-catering apartment be more suitable, especially if you are travelling in a group or with family? Do you plan to stay in one area or do you want to see many of the island's sights? If the latter, you may want to consider renting a car.

3 Choosing the Best Location
Where do you want to base your stay? In one of the bustling areas, a smaller village or a remote location? Such options exist by the sea, up in the mountains or on private *fincas* (ranches), either working farms or those that have been transformed into resorts.

4 Price
The cost of accommodation varies widely. You don't have to spend a great deal to find your desired location, but if you want to add luxuries and superb cuisine to your locale, there are far more costly choices too.

5 Making a Reservation
If you plan to visit in the warm months or during holidays, make reservations as far in advance as possible. The good-value accommodation fills up quickly, and even high-end gems can be booked solid in July and August. Confirm exact dates and type of accommodation with hotel management via email or fax.

6 Finding a Hotel on the Spot
Unless you want to spend hours casting about for a room, and possibly not finding anything in your price-range, this is not recommended, except in low season. Even then, bear in mind that many establishments close in winter. Also remember that there are no official tourist agencies that handle reservations, so your search may involve lots of footwork.

7 Tipping
As elsewhere in Europe, tipping is not absolutely necessary. Workers are paid living wages and should not depend on tips. However, a few coins for services rendered by the hotel staff are never amiss. You can tip porters and bellboys on the spot, and leave something for the maid in your room – or a general tip for all staff at the check-out desk.

8 Hidden Extras
A tax of 8% may or may not be included in the quoted price of your room; it is always best to ask or you could end up paying more than you expected. Parking, phone use and breakfast may or may not be charged as extra; determine what you are liable for in advance.

9 Travelling with Children
Mallorca is well set up for family travel. With very few exceptions, children are more than welcome at hotels and resorts, and those under certain ages may even stay free. Many hotels have a full schedule of special events and activities for kids, often at no extra charge. *(See also p134.)*

10 Language
With many decades of international tourism behind them, most Mallorcans are by now polyglots, and are likely to manage very well in English as well as other languages. However, it's a good idea to learn a little of the local lingo, Mallorquí (a dialect of Catalan) and Spanish, at least for getting around and pleasantries.

Left **Hotel Born, Palma** Right **San Lorenzo, Palma**

🔟 Historic Lodgings

1 Palacio Ca Sa Galesa, Palma

One of Mallorca's most lavish hotels, set in a 16th-century palace behind the Cathedral. Sumptuous period antiques and architectural features abound, including stained-glass bathrooms and huge Jacuzzis in some suites. 🚫 *C/Miramar, 8 • 971 715400 • www.palacio casagalesa.com • Limited dis acc • €€€€*

2 San Lorenzo, Palma

This 17th-century manor house in the medieval quarter of Palma has been restored with care, preserving its Mallorcan character while providing every creature comfort. Wrought iron, beamed ceilings, stone and tile accents create an elegant setting. You'll forget you're in the middle of a city. Free Wi-Fi. 🚫 *C/Sant Llorenç, 14 • 971 728200 • www.hotelsanlorenzo. com • Limited dis acc • €€€€*

3 Hotel Born, Palma

The 16th-century palace of the Marquis of Ferrandell has a classic Mallorcan courtyard entrance with palm trees, marble floors and Ionic columns. Oriental carpets and chandeliers are among other touches. Rooms are simple but comfortable and have autonomous air conditioning. 🚫 *C/Sant Jaume, 3 • 971 712942 • www.hotel born. com • No dis acc • €€€*

4 Gran Hotel Son Net, Puigpunyent

Set in a mountain-ringed valley, this 17th-century palace is filled with priceless antiques. The beautifully tended grounds feature a large pool, gym and tennis courts. Each room has a unique character. Free Wi-Fi. 🚫 *Map B3 • Castillo de Son Net • 971 147000 • www.sonnet.es • Limited dis acc • €€€€€*

5 Convent de la Missío, Palma

A 17th-century monastery has been sumptuously converted into a stylish boutique hotel. Minimalist furnishings in cool shades of white complement the historic setting. The former refectory is now an elegant restaurant. 🚫 *Map N2 • C/de la Missió, 7 • 971 227347 • www. conventdelamissio.com • Limited dis acc • €€€€€*

6 El Guia, Sóller

Modest old building with a thick atmosphere of yesteryear. A dining room hung with crystal chandeliers forms a wing of the ground floor. Rooms are basic, though. 🚫 *Map C2 • C/Castanyer, 2 • 971 630227 • www.sollernet. com/elguia • No dis acc • €€*

7 Hotel Juma, Pollença

On Pollença's central square, this Modernista hotel is full of antiques. Many rooms overlook the square; some have four-poster beds. Free Wi-Fi. 🚫 *Map E1 • Plaça Major, 9 • 971 535002 • www.hotel juma.com • No dis acc • €€€*

8 Hotel Sant Jaume, Alcúdia

Located in the old heart of Alcúdia, this 19th-century house has been beautifully renovated. There is a leafy courtyard garden with a fountain for summer, and a cozy lounge with an open fire for the cooler months. 🚫 *Map F2 • C/Sant Jaume, 6 • 971 549419 • www. hotelsantjaume.com • Closed Dec–Jan • Limited dis acc • €€*

9 Sa Plaça, Petra

There's a timeless feel to the elegant rooms: rough medieval walls with elaborate antiques and smooth Post-Modern touches. The effect is comfortable and original, accented by indirect lighting and lots of space. The serene restaurant is one of Mallorca's best (see p125). 🚫 *Map F4 • Plaça Ramon Llull, 4 • 971 561646 • Limited dis acc • €€€*

10 Leon de Sineu, Sineu

Behind the rather stark walls of this 500-year-old building, you'll find a delightful garden and spacious rooms with antiques and modern comforts. The area is great for discovering out-of-the-way places. 🚫 *Map E3 • C/Bous, 129 • 971 520211 • www.hotel-leondesineu. com • No dis acc • €€€*

Note: *Unless otherwise stated, all hotels accept credit cards, and have en-suite bathrooms and air conditioning*

Price Categories

For a standard, double room per night (with breakfast if included), taxes and extra charges.

€ under €50
€€ €50–€100
€€€ €100–€150
€€€€ €150–€200
€€€€€ over €200

Hotel Barceló Formentor

🔟 Resort Hotels

1 Villa Italia, Port d'Andratx

A gracious Italianate structure from the 1920s, with luxury suites or annex rooms. The restaurant is fabulous *(see p100)*. ⓈMap A4 • Camino de San Carlos, 13 • 971 674 011 • www.hotelvillaitalia.com • No dis acc • €€€€€

2 Hotel Es Port, Port de Sóller

A historic house and tower set in grounds with a spa, terraces, pools, tennis courts and fountains. Some rooms are in the modern annex, others are in the gardens, but the most atmospheric are in the old house. ⓈMap C2 • C/ Antonio Montis • 971 631 650 • www.hotelesport. com • No dis acc • €€€

3 Bacchus Read's, Santa Maria del Camí

Where else might a trompe-l'oeil lion gaze on you as you enjoy your Jacuzzi? Elegant yet unostentatious, this is Mallorcan resort living at its finest. The staff take an interest in your comfort. Its restaurant is one of Mallorca's best *(see pp83 & 125)*. Free Wi-Fi. ⓈMap D3 • Ctra. Vieja Santa María-Alaró • 971 140261 • www.readshotel.com • Limited dis acc • €€€€€

4 Hotel Rural Monnaber Nou

An old manor house amid age-old groves at the foot of the Serra de Tramuntana. Rough stone and stucco walls set off rich antiques and tapestries. ⓈMap E2 • Campanet • 971 877176 • www.monnaber.com • Dis acc • €€€€

5 Illa d'Or, Port de Pollença

Quiet and greenery reign at this 1920s pile by the water. Take a dip from the private beach or simply sip a drink and take in the magnificent views. ⓈMap E1 • Passeig Colón, 265 • 971 865100 • www.hoposa.es • €€€€

6 Hotel Barceló Formentor, Port de Pollença

It's the island's first and grandest resort, and the guest list is like a Who's Who of the 20th century: Churchill, the Windsors, Chaplin, Princess Grace, Placido Domingo, the Dalai Lama…. A spectacular setting, a private beach, lovely gardens, and every luxury you could wish for. *(see also pp29, 35 & 105).* ⓈMap E1 • 971 899100 • www.barceloformentor. com • €€€€€

7 La Reserva Rotana, Manacor

A meditative swing above the pool is reason enough to come. The rooms are huge, the service is enthusiastic, and the grounds include a golf course. ⓈMap F4 • Camí de S'Avall • 971 845685 • www.reservarotana.com • Limited dis acc • €€€€€

8 El Vistamar, Porto Colom

A fine complex of stylish modern buildings, four pools, various terraces, tennis courts, mini-golf, beauty centre, Turkish bath, gym, sauna and massage salon. There are entertainment programmes and personal therapists on hand. ⓈMap G5 • Hnos. Pinzón • 971 825101 • www.ola hotels.com • Dis acc • €€€

9 Hotel Rural Sa Bassa Rotja, Porreres

The pace of life slows within this remote, vineclad mansion, dating from the 13th century. Guest rooms are invitingly decorated in warm tones and luxurious fabrics. All the usual resort facilities are included. ⓈMap E4 • Finca Son Orell, Camino Sa Pedrera • 971 168225 • www.sa bassarotja.com • Limited dis acc • €€€€

10 Tres Playas, Colònia de Sant Jordi

Terrace after terrace descends to the sea, punctuated with beautiful gardens and pools along the way. Many activities are on offer, including aqua classes, water polo and tennis. All of the spacious rooms have sea views and balconies, and some of Mallorca's finest beaches are nearby. There are also bars, restaurants and a beauty salon. ⓈMap E6 • C/Esmeralda • 971 655151 • €€€€

Note: Mallorca is primarily a summer destination and many establishments close for a few months in winter (usually Nov–Mar)

Left **Mirabo** Right **Gran Hotel Son Julia**

Boutique Hotels

1 Scott's, Binissalem

Located in the heart of Binissalem, this 19th-century mansion has been lovingly renovated. Enjoy the peaceful lounge, library and extensive gardens. ◎ Map D3 • Plaza de la Iglesia, 12 • 971 870100 • www.scottshotel.com • Ltd dis acc • €€€€€

2 Hospes Maricel, Palma

This 17th-century palace is full of modern features, such as a large infinity pool, a spa and wellness centre and an excellent restaurant. All the rooms have king-size beds and plasma TVs. ◎ Map R2 • Ctra. D'Andratx, 11 (MA-1c), Calvià • 971 707744 • www.hospes.es • Dis acc • €€€€€

3 Mirabo, Valldemossa

The work of architect Frank Lloyd Wright inspired the renovation of this country house overlooking Valldemossa. Only the number of rooms and the infinity pool detract from the impression that it might be an artist's home. ◎ Map C3 • Ctra. Valldemossa Km15 • 661 285215 • www.mirabo.es • Dis acc • €€€€€

4 Finca Ca N'Ai, Sóller

Owned by a local family for 14 generations, this country estate has been converted into a delightful hotel. Luxurious suites are clustered around the old house. ◎ Map C2 • Cami Son Sales, 50 • 971 632494 • www.canai.com • Ltd dis acc • €€€€€

5 Casa del Virrey, Inca

This grand, country mansion expertly combines period details with modern amenities. The public spaces, decorated with antiques and unusual artworks, retain their original features, such as marble fireplaces. ◎ Map E3 • Carretera Inca-Sencelles km2, 4 • 971 881018 • www.casadelvirrey.net • Ltd dis acc • €€€

6 Son Brull, Pollença

Rural style sits alongside avant garde design in this charming hotel. Rooms and suites have modern facilities, and there are sports activities on offer. The restaurant specializes in Mallorcan cuisine and gives cookery classes too. Free Wi-Fi. ◎ Map E1 • Ctra. Palma-Pollenca, km 50 • 971 535353 • www.sonbrull.com • Closed Dec–Jan • Dis acc • €€€€€

7 Desbrull, Pollença

This attractive town house blends period style with modern design. The public spaces are decorated with local art (some of which is for sale). The contemporary feel continues to the six suites, which have ultra-modern bathrooms. ◎ Map E1 • Marquès Desbrull, 7 • 971 535055 • www.desbrull.com • Closed Dec–Jan • Dis acc • €€€

8 Cas Ferrer Nou Hotelet, Alcúdia

This cosmopolitan hotel has been beautifully decorated. Each of the six rooms and suites has its own unique theme inspired by different areas of the Mediterranean. Free Wi-Fi. ◎ Map F2 • Carrer Pou Nou 1 • 971 897542 • www.nouhotelet.com • Ltd dis acc • €€€

9 Son Cleda, Binissalem

The comfortable rooms of this delightful town house have been traditionally designed, but are equipped with modern amenities. The restaurant-café has a pretty terrace, which is the perfect place to enjoy the warm sunshine and lovely view. Free Wi-Fi. ◎ Map E3 • Plaça es Fossar 7, Sineu • 971 521038 • www.hotelsoncleda.com • Ltd dis acc • €€

10 Gran Hotel Son Julia, Llucmajmor

Housed in an opulent 19th-century mansion, this hotel is one of the best in Mallorca. There are a variety of rooms, but the most luxurious is the Imperial Suite, with its own lounge, walk-in shower, Jacuzzi and mini-gym. ◎ Map D5 • Crta. S'Arenal-Llucmajor s/n • 971 669700 • www.sonjulia.com • Dis acc • €€€€€

Note: Unless otherwise stated, all hotels accept credit cards, and have en-suite bathrooms and air conditioning

Price Categories

For a standard, double room per night (with breakfast if included), taxes and extra charges.

€ under €50
€€ €50–€100
€€€ €100–€150
€€€€ €150–€200
€€€€€ over €200

La Residencia

TOP 10 Mountain Retreats

1 Es Molí, Deià
The eagle's retreat par excellence. Rooms are traditional and comfortable (those in the annex are cheaper), and there is use of a pool, tennis court and private beach. ✎ Map C2 • Ctra. Valldemossa-Deià • 971 639000 • www. esmoli.com • Limited dis acc • €€€€€

2 La Residencia, Deià
The huge 18th-century manor house dominates the entire Deià valley, rising high above the road and affording unparalleled views of the sea and encircling mountains. Very popular with the rich and famous, who love to be pampered here in perfect privacy. Free Wi-Fi. ✎ Map C2 • Son Canals s/n • 971 639011 • www. hotel-laresidencia.com • Limited dis acc • €€€€€

3 Costa d'Or, Deià
A quaint cluster of rough stone buildings set against verdant rocky promontories, this quality hotel provides simple yet comfortable accommodation. Features include a lovely pine grove, abundant gardens, a pool, tennis court and minigolf. ✎ Map C2 • Lluc-Alcari • 971 639025 • Apr–Oct • www.hoposa.es • Limited dis acc • €€€€

4 Ca's Xorc, Sóller
Located above the Sóller Valley, eye-to-eye with the Serra de Tramuntana, this elegant country house offers a majestic pool and breathtaking views. Original artwork and sumptuous Moroccan-style touches create a sense of pure luxury. It also has one of the best restaurants in the area (see p82). ✎ Map C2 • Carretera Sóller-Deià, km 56.1 • 971 638280 • www.casxorc.com • Limited dis acc • €€€€€

5 Can'Aí, Sóller
The shady orange groves and small canals surrounding this ancient manor house date back to Arab times. The incomparable setting, in a silent valley ringed with mountains, provides all the serenity guests seek. Charming, unique rooms. ✎ Map C2 • Camí de son Sales, 50, Sóller • 971 632 494 • www.canai.com • Limited dis acc • €€€

6 C'an Reus, Fornalutx
Rustic yet elegant, filled with a mix of plain furniture and period antiques. There's a simple pool in the garden, and stunning views of the precipitous valley and mountains. ✎ Map C2 • C/l'Auba, 26, Fornalutx • 971 631174 • www.canreushotel.com • No dis acc • €€€

7 Ca'n Verdera, Fornalutx
Sophia Loren has stayed in this chic and modern remodelling of a huge old house. Free Wi-Fi. ✎ Map D2 • C/des Toros, 1 • 971 638203 • www.canverdera. com • Limited dis acc • €€€€€

8 Can Furiós Petit Hotel, Binibona
A delightful 16th-century villa has been transformed into a mountain eyrie with gardens, terraces, shaded patios and an inviting pool. Rooms are richly decorated, several with antique canopy beds, and the restaurant is excellent. ✎ Map E2 • Camí Vell Binibona, 11, Caimari • 971 515751 • www.can-furios.com • No dis acc • €€€€

9 Finca Son Mola Vell, Son Macià
This beautifully restored country house has a pool, sauna and other luxuries. Dine on the terrace in summer, enjoying sunset views along with the great food. ✎ Map F4 • Ctra. Son Macià-Cales de Mallorca, km 2.8 • 971 554664 • Limited dis acc • €€€

10 Finca Son Sama, Llucmajor
The manor house, built in 1531, retains its rancho feel. Objects from centuries ago punctuate the gardens, and the secluded setting is one of great beauty. Rooms and baths are spacious, there's a great restaurant, Es Mirador (see p125), and a riding school attached. ✎ Map D5 • Ctra. Llucmajor-Porreres, km 3.5 • 971 120959 • www.sonsama. com • No dis acc • €€

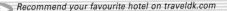

Left **Hostal Playa** Right **Hostal Nereida**

Seaside Charmers

Hotel Petit, Cala Fornells

High over the scenic bay, with panoramic views and several levels of terraces with splashing fountains, this little gem offers all the amenities of a resort. The decor is a simple blend of traditional Spanish and Moroccan. There are four pools, a small secluded beach and a cove. ⊗ *Map B4 • 971 685 405 • www.petitcalafornells.com • Limited dis acc • €€€€€*

Hotel Brisas, Port de Sóller

Small, unpretentious and atmospheric, this simple establishment is located at the quiet end of the west side of the port. Recently renovated, the rooms are plain, but all come with their own balconies offering splendid views. ⊗ *Map C2 • Camino del Faro, 15 • 971 631352 • No dis acc • €€*

Hotel Cala Sant Vicenç

This handsome hotel is surrounded by lush gardens. Classically elegant rooms offer every comfort and there are two superb restaurants as well as a snack bar by the pool. ⊗ *Map E1 • C/Maressers, 2 • 971 530 250 • www. hotelcala.com • Dis acc • €€€€€*

Hotel Can Simoneta, Canyamel

This 150-year old finca is surrounded by fragrant gardens and perched serenely on a cliff top overlooking coves and turquoise waters. Rooms boast wooden beams, four-poster beds and contemporary furnishings. ⊗ *Map H3 • Ctra Arta-Canyamel, km 8 • 971 816110 • www.cansimoneta. com • Dis acc • €€€€€*

Hostal Bahia, Port de Pollença

Appealing period building with shutters and a sea-front patio, surrounded by gardens and pines. The views are excellent, and the mood relaxed and friendly. Rooms are gracious and spacious, many with terraces, beamed ceilings and interesting antiques here and there. ⊗ *Map E1 • Passeig Voramar • 971 866562 • www.hoposa.es • Limited dis acc • €€*

Miramar, Port de Pollença

A stylish establishment, with beamed ceilings, a terrace with a sea view, and lush gardens. Its elegant patios are graced with antiques and ceramics, and the rooms are quiet and comfortable. ⊗ *Map E1 • Passeig Anglada Camarassa, 39 • 971 866400 • www. hotel-miramar.net • Limited dis acc • €€€*

Hotel Uyal, Port de Pollença

Very charming, Spanish-style elegance right on the beachfront. Arches and beams define the lovely rooms. ⊗ *Map E1 • Paseo Londres • 971 865500 • www.hoposa.es • No dis acc • €€€*

Hostal Nereida, Porto Petro

It's the only hotel in town! There's a warm family feeling, a large garden, big swimming pool, children's park, tennis and an excellent restaurant. Rooms are simple, all with balcony, some with views. ⊗ *Map F6 • C/Patrons Martina, 3 • 971 657223 • www.hostalnereida.com • No dis acc • €€*

Hotel Lemar, Colònia San Jordi

A palpable colonial feel, with rattan furniture and ceiling fans. Many balconies enjoy great views of the beach and turquoise sea. Mostly German clientele. ⊗ *Map E6 • C/Gabriel Roca, 55 • 971 655178 • www.hotellemar. com • Limited dis acc • €€*

Hostal Playa, Colònia Sant Jordi

Adorably old-fashioned and just a little bit funky, this secret hideaway has a wonderful patio-terrace on a practically private beach, composed of sand and large flat rocks. Old ceramics decorate every room, enhancing the white-washed, red-tiled character of the place. ⊗ *Map E6 • C/Major, 25 • 971 655256 • www. restauranteplaya.com • No dis acc • €€*

Note: *Unless otherwise stated, all hotels accept credit cards, and have en-suite bathrooms and air conditioning*

Price Categories

For a standard, double room per night (with breakfast if included), taxes and extra charges.	€€ under €50 €€ €50–€100 €€€ €100–€150 €€€€ €150–€200 €€€€€ over €200

Left **Relaxing by the pool at Sa Pedrissa, Deià** Right **Raïms sign**

🔟 Agroturismo (Farmhouses)

1 Son Esteve, Andratx

Dating back to 903, this picturesque structure was built by the Moors. Service is attentive, the rooms are comfortable and there is a lovely pool – all just minutes from the old town and port. A lavish breakfast with homemade yogurt and jams is included. ◎ Map B4 • Camí Ca's Vidals, 42 • 655 572630 • www.sonesteve. com • Limited dis acc • €€€

2 Sa Pedrissa, Deià

Surrounded by ancient olive trees and blessed with fabulous sea views, this 16th-century country estate has been restored to the standards of the best hotels, without losing its historic appeal. Dine on local cuisine in the beautiful converted olive press room. ◎ Map C2 • Ctra. Valldemossa-Deià, km 64.5 • 971 639111 • www.sapedrissa.com • Limited dis acc • €€€€€

3 Ca's Curial, Sóller

You get a lot of space and luxury for the price. There's a rustic feel and antiques but also every modern amenity, all set in a fragrant orange grove just a few minutes from central Sóller. The views of the jagged, pine-covered mountains are stunning, as you sit around the pool on the shaded terrace. ◎ Map C2 • C/La Villalonga, 23 • 971 633332 • www.cascurial.com • Limited dis acc • €€€€

4 Ca'n Moragues, Artá

A small and exclusive hotel set in a refurbished 18th-century manor house in the heart of Artá. Every comfort has been seen to in the unique combination of antique and modern furnishings. ◎ Map G3 • C/Pou Nou, 12 • 971 829509 • www.canmoragues.com • Limited dis acc • €€€

5 Son Gener, Son Severa

Exquisite 18th-century country estate with charm and personalized service. The cooking is top-notch, and all of the sleek rooms are junior suites. There's a patio, pool, terraces and spa. ◎ Map G3 • Ctra. Vieja Son Servera-Artà, km 3 • 971 183612 • www.songener.com • Closed Dec–mid-Jan • Limited dis acc • €€€€€

6 Mayolet, Manacor

Attached to the Reserva Rotana, whose pool it shares, this old farmer's stone house has been updated for every comfort. The rooms are large and rustic, and like a home-from-home. ◎ Map F4 • Camí de S'Arall, km 3 • 971 845685 • www.mayolet.com • Limited dis acc • €€€

7 Sa Carrotja, Ses Salines

The 17th-century farmhouse has been modernized without losing any of its country charms, a place where you can sample local cuisine made from the proprietor's own organic produce. A quiet, refined choice, but not really suitable for children. ◎ Map E6 • Sa Carrotja, 7 • 971 649053 • www.sacarrotja.com • No dis acc • €€€

8 Ses Rotes Velles, Campos–Colònia Sant Jordi

Immaculate lawns set off beautiful flower gardens, a vibrant counterpoint to the rich ochre of the bungalows. The food is some of the island's best. ◎ Ctra. Campos-Colonia Sant Jordi, km 8.7 • 971 656159 • www.agroturismosesrotesvelles.com • Limited dis acc • €€€

9 Raïms, Algaida

The self catering apartments are modern, but this country house has kept its old wine cellars and stone floors. A sense of timelessness settles over everything as you laze by the pool. ◎ Map D4 • C/Ribera, 24 • 971 665 157 • www.finca-raims.com • Limited dis acc • €€€

10 Sa Torre, Santa Eugènia

The 13th-century estate is surrounded by wheat fields, close to the island's agricultural centre. The old wine cellar has been converted into an inviting restaurant. All rooms are spacious apartments. ◎ Map D3 • C/Alqueries, 70 • 971 144011 • www.sa-torre.com • Limited dis acc • €€€

Left **Castell d'Alaró, near hostel** Right **Santuari de Sant Salvador**

TOP 10 Monasteries, Refuges and Hostels

1 Refugi Can Boi, Deià

This comfortable refuge offers 32 beds, hot water and food. Towels and bed linen can be rented on site. Reservations must be made a minimum of five days in advance. A number of walks can be taken from the refuge. ◎ *Map C2 • C/des Clot, 5 • 971 173731 • www.conselldemallorca.cat • No dis acc • No credit cards • No air con • €*

2 Castell d'Alaró

The hostel is a 45-minute walk from the scenic castle (see p97). There are double and triple rooms, a communal room and snack bar, but facilities are otherwise modest: come prepared with whatever you might require. ◎ *Map D3 • Puig d'Alaró • 971 182112 • No dis acc • No credit cards • No en-suite • No air con • €*

3 Refugio Tossals Verds, Lloseta

It's a one hour walk from the Clot d'Almendra to this place, which gives access to the highest summits of the range. The house, an old mountain construction, has been modernized with an en-suite double room and two rooms with bunks for 8 and 12 people. There is heating, and guests can cook their own meals or eat at the restaurant. ◎ *Map D3 • Finca Tossals Verds • 971 173731 • No dis acc • Not all en-suite • No air con • €*

4 Santuari de Lluc

In this most famous of Mallorca's retreats (see pp26–7), you'll find considerable comfort and every sort of facility, including outside tables, barbecue areas, bars and restaurants, and camping possibilities. The accommodation is closer to hotel-style than most such retreats on the island. ◎ *Map D2 • 971 517096 • www.lluc.net • Limited dis acc • No air con • €*

5 Santuari del Puig de Maria, Pollença

High on the Puig de Maria. There's a kitchen with a coal fire, and a dining room with a fireplace and restaurant. Bathrooms are communal, and only one of the showers has hot water (see p60). ◎ *Map E1 • 971 184132 • No dis acc • No credit cards • No en-suite • No air con • €*

6 Santuari de Cura, Randa

Set in verdant, peaceful gardens on the peak of the Puig de Randa, this historic sanctuary offers lovely views of the island. It has been beautifully restored, and the rooms are comfortable and well equipped. ◎ *Map E4 • Randa, 07629 • 971 120260 • No credit cards • No air con • €€*

7 Ermita de Bonany, Petra

Set in a Special Interest Nature Area. The five rooms share communal showers, a kitchen, dining room and outside barbecue areas (bring your own BBQ) with picnic tables. ◎ *Map F4 • Puig de Bonany • 971 826568 • No dis acc • No en-suite • No air con • €*

8 Santuari de Monti-Sion, Porreres

The very simple amenities here are reminiscent of the asceticism of yesteryear. The 16th-century lecture hall is preserved, as are four Gothic pillars on the path that ascends from the village to the summit. Great views of the entire Central Plain. ◎ *Map E4 • Oratori de Monti-Sion • 971 647185 • No dis acc • No credit cards • No air con • €*

9 Santuari de Sant Salvador, Felanitx

Modest accommodations and amenities include hot water, a kitchen, dining room, barbecue areas, picnic tables, and a bar and restaurant (see p61). ◎ *Map F5 • Pl. Santa Margarita, 6 • 971 827282 • No dis acc • No credit cards • No air con • €*

10 Youth Hostels

There are two official hostels in barracks-like buildings. Book in advance, as they get full quickly. ◎ *Albergue Platja de Palma, C/Costa Brava, 13, outside Palma (closed Nov–Feb) • Albergue de la Victòria, Ctra. Cap Pinar, km 4.9, north of Alcúdia • 902 111188 (for both) • €*

For more about Mallorca's religious sanctuaries and hermitages see pp60–61

Price Categories

For a standard, double room per night (with breakfast if included), taxes and extra charges.

€	under €50
€€	€50–€100
€€€	€100–€150
€€€€	€150–€200
€€€€€	over €200

Hotel Marina, Port de Sóller

◨10 Self-Catering Apartments

1 Apartamentos Cala Viñas, Palma Bay

Stepped, Meso-American style, with red tile roofs and ample balconies, this complex of hotel rooms and apartments is built on a rocky prominence at one end of the Bay of Palma. Close to beach. ✆ Map Q3 • C/Las Sirenas, 17, Calvià • 971 130982 • www.hihotels.net • Limited dis acc • €€€€

2 Aldea Cala Fornells I, Peguera Bay

Attractive bungalows scattered along a hillside, near shops and other services, all overlooking the gorgeous bay. There's a large pool for guests' use, and nearby you'll find tennis, horse riding and every watersport. All rentals are one-bedroom, one bath, and sleep up to four persons. ✆ Map B4 • Ctra Cala Fornells (Peguera) • 971 686920 • www.aldeai.com • Limited dis acc • Not all with air con • €€

3 Ca's Curial, Sóller

This agroturismo/finca (farmhouse/ranch) in the heart of the beautiful Sóller Valley, has two rental properties with all facilities, one that sleeps six, one for eight. A pool, patios and terraces are reserved for guests' use. The area is excellent for walking. ✆ Map C2 • C/La Villalonga, 23, Sóller • 971 633332 • www.cascurial.com Limited dis acc • €€€€

4 Hotel Marina, Port de Sóller

On a palm-lined, pedestrianized area, this simple apartment-hotel enjoys great views, and a superb beach is just outside the front door. The decor features terracotta tile floors, and every room has good-sized balconies. ✆ Map C2 • Paseo La Playa, Platja d'En Repic • 971 634182 • www.hotel marinasoller.com • Limited dis acc • €€

5 Hotel Generoso, Port de Sóller

Right on the beach by the picturesque Sóller tramline, with views of the port and mountains from the upper floors. Rooms are small and simple, but have balconies and often marble floors and walls. There's a pool, solarium, bar and restaurant. ✆ Map C2 • Calle Marina, 4 • 971 631450 • www.hotelgeneroso.com • Limited dis acc • €€

6 Finca Ca'n Sagra, Pollença

Large mountain chalet with 1,000-year-old olive trees, a pool, vast terraces and breathtaking views. You get an American-style kitchen, a pool house with bathroom, barbecue, central heating, golf and shops nearby, and the whole place is furnished with genuine antiques. ✆ Map E1 • 639 441672 • www.als-mallorca.com • Limited dis acc • Not all with air con • €€€€€ (min one-week stay)

7 Apartamentos Oro Playa, Port de Pollença

In a quiet location near the beach, marina and town centre, these apartments are ideal for families. Lush gardens include a playground and pool. ✆ Map E1 • Ctra de Formentor s/n • 971 864441 • www.marhotels.com • €€€

8 Coco's House, Port de Pollença

These apartments are located amid pines on a picturesque curve of the bay, near shops and scintillating nightlife. ✆ Map E1 • C/Pescador, 44 • 653 359950 • www.cocoshouse.co.uk • No dis acc • €€

9 Apartamentos Bouganvilla, Zona de Sa Coma

Low-rise bungalows on a limpid cove. The design is traditional Spanish, with arches, balconies and terraces. ✆ Map G4 • C/Margarita, 1 • 971 810348 • www.hihotels.net • Limited dis acc • €€€

10 Es Pla de Llodrà, Manacor

A beautifully renovated finca that has been converted into three apartments, sleeping between two and four. There is an outdoor pool set in extensive gardens. ✆ Map F4 • Ctra Manacor–Felanitx km 4.5 • 610 634 697 • www.espladellodra.com • No dis acc • €€

Price categories for self-catering apartments apply to a typical unit per night – check to see how many people the unit sleeps

147

General Index

Acknowledgements

The Author
Jeffrey Kennedy is a freelance travel writer who divides his time between the Iberian Peninsula, Italy and the USA. He is the author of Dorling Kindersley's *Top 10 Miami* and *Top 10 San Francisco* and co-author of *Top 10 Rome*.

The author would like to thank María Andersson, Maria Casanovas i Codina, Jolie Chain, Tomeu Deyà, Oriol Galgo, Marr Goodrum, Britta Ploenzke, Anna Skidmore, Mike Suarez and Concha Tejada.

Produced by BLUE ISLAND PUBLISHING, LONDON
www.blueisland.co.uk

Editorial Director
Rosalyn Thiro

Art Director
Stephen Bere

Associate Editor
Michael Ellis

Designer
Lee Redmond

Picture Research
Ellen Root

Research Assistance
Amaia Allende

Proofreader
Jane Simmonds

Fact-checker
Paula Canal

Indexer
Jane Simmonds

Main Photographer
Colin Sinclair

Additional Photography
Joe Cornish, Neil Mersh, David Murray and Jules Selmes, Clive Streeter, Barteomines Zaranek, Stephen Bere.

Cartography
Martin Darlison Tom Coulson (Encompass Graphics Ltd)
Source data for Mallorca derived from Netmaps.
www.netmaps.es

AT DORLING KINDERSLEY

Publisher
Douglas Amrine

Publishing Manager
Fay Franklin

Senior Art Editor
Marisa Renzullo

Senior Cartographic Editor
Casper Morris

DTP
Jason Little,
Conrad van Dyk

Production
Melanie Dowland

Additional Assistance
Marta Bescos, Tessa Bindloss, Andrea Boyd, Sherry Collins, Emer FitzGerald, Karen Fitzpatrick, Fay Franklin, Anna Freiberger, Rhiannon Furbear, John Gill, Lydia Halliday, Juliet Kenny, Priya Kukadia, Neil Lockley, Quadrum Solutions, Ellen Root

Photography Permissions
Dorling Kindersley would like to thank all the cathedrals, churches, museums, hotels, restaurants, bars, clubs, shops, galleries and other sights for their assistance and kind permission to photograph at their establishments.

Placement Key: t = top; tl = top left; tr = top right; tc = top centre; c = centre; cr = centre right; b= bottom; bl = bottom left; br = bottom right. Works of art have been reproduced with the permission of the following copyright holders:

Courtesy of Fundació Pilar i Joan Miró: all 14, 14–15, 62tc, 88br

Joan Oliver Fuster 20b

Joan Miró © ADAGP, Paris and DACS, London 14b, 63t

MUSEO D'ART ESPANYOL CONTEMPORANI: Guillermo Pérez Villalta La Estancia 62c

The publisher would like to thank the following individuals, companies and picture libraries for their kind permission to reproduce their photographs in this publication:

A1Pix: 52t; AISA-BCN: 35tr; ALAMY IMAGES: S. Forster 99tl; Francisco Martinez 119t

PEDRO CAUBET: 32–33; CHIVAS: 73t; CORBIS: Archivo Iconografico 35tl, 35br; Bettmann 35cr; Cordaiy Photo Library Ltd/Chris North 52c; CONVENT DE LA MISSIO: 82cla; COVER: C. Agustin 53tl;

J. Echevarria 53bl; Ramon Rabal 32b; COVES DEL DRAC: 32t, 33t, 33b

DISCOTECA MENTA: 109tr

EL LOFT EDITORIAL: 99tr

FUNDACIÓ PILAR I JOAN MIRÓ: 6bl, 15t, 15b

GALLERIES VINCENÇ, S.A.U.107tc; GRAN CASINO DE MALLORCA: 72tr, 72b; GRAN HOTEL SON JULIA: 142tr; LA GRANJA DE ESPORLAS; 17cb

HOSPITAL UNIVERSITARI SON DURETA: 131tr; HOSTAL RESTAURANTE PLAYA: 144tl; HOTEL ARIES: 76tc; HOTEL LEON DE SINEU: 125tc; HOTEL MARINA 7 APARTAMENTOS MARINA PLAYA; 147tl

LOEWE; 70tr

ROBERT MACKAY: 76tl; MALLORCA RESTAURANTS-121: 117tr; MIRABO HOTEL: 142tl; MUSEU DE LLUC; Toni Málaga 27ca

NHPA: Julia Meech 38tl; Roger Tidman 38c, 38b

PURO HOTEL: 73br

All other images are © Dorling Kindersley. For more information see www.dkimages.com

Special Editions of DK Travel Guides

DK Travel Guides can be purchased in bulk quantities at discounted prices for use in promotions or as premiums. We are also able to offer special editions and personalized jackets, corporate imprints, and excerpts from all of our books, tailored specifically to meet your own needs.

To find out more, please contact:
(in the United States) SpecialSales@dk.com
(in the UK) travelspecialsales @uk.dk.com
(in Canada) DK Special Sales at general@tourmaline.ca
(in Australia) business.development @pearson.com.au

English-Mallorquín Phrase Book

In an Emergency

Help!	**Auxili!**	ow-**gzee**-lee
Stop!	**Pareu!**	**pah**-reh-oo
Call a doctor!	**Telefoneu un**	teh-leh-fon-**eh**-oo
	metge!	oon **meh**-djuh
Call an	**Telefoneu una**	teh-leh-fon-**eh**-oo
ambulance!	**ambulància!**	oo-nah ahm-boo-**lahn**-see-ah
Call the police!	**Telefoneu**	teh-leh-fon-**eh**-oo
	la policia	lah poh-lee-**see**-ah
Call the fire	**Telefoneu**	teh-leh-fon-**eh**-oo
brigade!	**els bombers!**	uhlz boom-**behs**
Where is the	**On és**	**on**-ehs uhl tuh-leh-
nearest	**el teléfon**	**fon** mehs
telephone?	**més proper?**	proo-**peh**
Where is the	**On és**	**on**-ehs looss-pee-
nearest	**l'hospital**	**tahl** mehs
hospital?	**més proper?**	proo-**peh**

Communication Essentials

Yes	**Sí**	see
No	**No**	noh
Please	**Si us plau**	sees plah-oo
Thank you	**Gràcies**	**grah**-see-uhs
Excuse me	**Perdoni**	puhr-**thoh**-nee
Hello	**Hola**	**oh**-lah
Goodbye	**Adéu**	ah-they-**oo**
Good night	**Bona nit**	**bo**-nah neet
Morning	**El matí**	uhl muh-**tee**
Afternoon	**La tarda**	lah **tahr**-thuh
Evening	**El vespre**	uhl **vehs**-pruh
Yesterday	**Ahir**	ah-**ee**
Today	**Avui**	uh-voo-**ee**
Tomorrow	**Demà**	duh-**mah**
Here	**Aquí**	uh-**kee**
There	**Allà**	uh-**lyah**
What?	**Qué?**	keh
When?	**Quan?**	**Kwahn**
Why?	**Per qué?**	puhr keh
Where?	**On?**	ohn

Useful Phrases

How are you?	**Com està?**	kom uhs-**tah**
Very well,	**Molt bé,**	mol **beh**
thank you.	**gràcies.**	**grah**-see-uhs
Pleased to	**Molt de gust.**	mol duh **goost**
meet you.		
See you soon.	**Fins aviat.**	feenz uhv-**yat**
That's fine.	**Està bé.**	uhs-**tah** beh
Where is/are … ?	**On és/són...?**	ohn ehs/sohn
How far is it to … ?	**Quants metres/**	kwahnz meh-
	kilòmetres hi	truhs/kee-**loh**-
	ha d'aquí a … ?	muh-truhs dah-**kee** uh
Which	**Per on es**	puhr **on** uhs
way to … ?	**va a … ?**	**bah** ah
Do you speak	**Parla**	**par**-luh
English?	**anglés?**	an-**glehs**
I don't understand	**No l'entenc.**	noh luhn-**teng**

Useful Words

Could you	**Pot parlar més**	pot par-**lah** mehs
speak more	**a poc a poc,**	pok uh pok
slowly, please?	**si us plau?**	sees plah-oo
I'm sorry.	**Ho sento.**	oo **sehn**-too

Useful Words

big	**gran**	gran
small	**petit**	puh-**teet**
hot	**calent**	kah-**len**
cold	**fred**	fred
good	**bo**	boh
bad	**dolent**	doo-**len**
enough	**bastant**	bahs-**tan**
well	**bé**	beh
open	**obert**	oo-**behr**
closed	**tancat**	tan-**kat**
left	**esquerra**	uhs-**kehr**-ruh
right	**dreta**	**dreh**-tuh
straight on	**recte**	**rehk**-tuh
near	**a prop**	uh prop
far	**lluny**	**lyoon**yuh
up/over	**a dalt**	uh **dahl**
down/under	**a baix**	uh **bah**-eeshh
early	**aviat**	uhv-**yat**
late	**tard**	**tahrt**
entrance	**entrada**	uhn-**trah**-thuh
exit	**sortida**	**soor**-tee-thuh
toilet	**lavabos/**	luh-**vah**-boos
	serveis	sehr-**beh**-ees
more	**més**	mess
less	**menys**	**men**yees

Shopping

How much	**Quant**	kwahn
does this cost?	**costa això?**	kost ehs-**shoh**
I would like …	**M'agradaria …**	muh-**grah**-thuh-**ree**-ah
Do you have?	**Tenen?**	**tehn**-un
I'm just looking,	**Només estic**	noo -mess
thank you	**mirant, gràcies.**	ehs-**teek** mee-**rahn** **grah**-see-uhs
Do you take	**Accepten**	ak-**sehp**-tuhn
credit cards?	**targes de**	tahr-**zhuhs** duh
	crèdit?	**kreh**-deet
What time	**A quina hora**	ah **keen**-uh **oh**-ruh
do you open?	**obren?**	**oh**-bruhn
What time	**A quina hora**	ah **keen**-uh oh
do you close?	**tanquen?**	ruh **tan**-kuhn
This one.	**Aquest**	ah-**ket**
That one.	**Aquell**	ah-**kehl**
expensive	**car**	kahr
cheap	**bé de preu/**	beh thuh **preh**-oo/bah-**rat**
	barat	
size (clothes)	**talla/mida**	**tah**-lyah/**mee**-thuh
size (shoes)	**número**	**noo**-mehr-oo
white	**blanc**	blang
black	**negre**	**neh**-gruh
red	**vermell**	vuhr-**mel**
yellow	**groc**	grok

green	**verd**	**behrt**
blue	**blau**	**blah**-oo
antiques shop	**antiquari/ botiga d'antiguitats**	an-tee-**kwah**-ree/ boo-**tee**-gah/dan-**tee**-ghee-**tats**
bakery	**el forn**	uhl **forn**
bank	**el banc**	uhl **bang**
bookshop	**la llibreria**	lah lyee-bruh-**ree**-ah
butcher's	**la carnisseria**	lah kahr-nee-suh-**ree**-uh
fishmonger's	**la peixateria**	lah peh-shuh-tuh-**ree**-uh
greengrocer's	**la fruiteria**	lah froo-ee-tuh-**ree**-uh
grocer's	**la botiga de queviures**	lah boo-**tee**-guh duh keh-vee-**oo**-ruhs
hairdresser's	**la perruqueria**	lah peh-roo-kuh-**ree**-uh
market	**el mercat**	uhl muhr-**kat**
newsagent's	**el quiosc de premsa**	uhl kee-**ohsk** duh **prem**-suh
pastry shop	**la pastisseria**	lah pahs-tee-suh-**ree**-uh
pharmacy	**la farmàcia**	lah fuhr-**mah**-see-ah
post office	**l'oficina de correus**	loo-fee-**see**-nuh duh koo-**reh**-oos
shoe shop	**la sabateria**	lah sah-bah-tuh-**ree**-uh
supermarket	**el supermercat**	uhl soo-puhr-muhr-**kat**
tobacconist's	**l'estanc**	luhs-**tang**
travel agency	**l'agència de viatges**	la-**jen**-see-uh duh vee-**ad**-juhs

Sightseeing

art gallery	**la galeria d'art**	lah gah-luh-**ree**-yuh **dart**
cathedral	**la catedral**	lah kuh-tuh-**thrahl**
church	**l'església/ la basílica**	luhz-**gleh**-zee-uh/ lah buh-**zee**-lee-kuh
garden	**el jardí**	uhl zhahr-**dee**
library	**la biblioteca**	lah bee-blee-oo-**teh**-kuh
museum	**el museu**	uhl moo-**seh**-oo
tourist information office	**l'oficina de turisme**	loo-fee-**see**-nuh thuh too-**reez**-muh
town hall	**l'ajuntament**	luh-djoon-tuh-**men**
closed for holiday	**tancat per vacances**	tan-**kat** puhr bah-**kan**-suhs
bus station	**l'estació d'autobusos**	luhs-tah-see-**oh** dow-toh-**boo**-zoos
railway station	**l'estació de tren**	luhs-tah-see-**oh** thuh **tren**

Staying in a Hotel

Do you have a vacant room?	**Tenen una habitació lliure?**	**teh**-nuhn **oo**-nuh ah-bee-tuh-see-**oh lyuh**-ruh
double room with double bed	**habitació doble amb llit de matrimoni**	ah-bee-tuh-see-**oh doh**-bluh am **lyeet** duh mah-tree-**moh**-nee
twin room	**habitació amb dos llits/ amb llits individuals**	ah-bee-tuh-see-**oh** am **dohs lyeets**/ am **lyeets** in-thee-vee-thoo-**ahls**
single room	**habitació individual**	ah-bee-tuh-see-**oh** een-dee-vee-thoo-**ahl**
room with a bath shower	**habitació amb bany dutxa**	ah-bee-tuh-see-**oh** am **bah**nyuh **doo**-chuh
porter	**el grum**	uhl **groom**
key	**la clau**	lah **klah**-oo
I have a reservation	**Tinc una habitació reservada**	**ting oo**-nuh ah-bee-tuh-see-**oh** reh-sehr-**vah**-thah

Eating Out

Have you got a table for ...	**Tenen taula per...?**	**teh**-nuhn **tow**-luh puhr
I would like to reserve a table	**Voldria reservar una taula.**	vool-**dree**-uh reh-sehr-**vahr oo**-nuh **tow**-luh
The bill, please	**El compte, si us plau.**	uhl **kohm**-tuh sees plah-oo
I am a vegetarian.	**Sóc vegetarià/ vegetariana.**	**sok** buh-zhuh-tuh-ree-**ah** buh-zhuh-tuh-ree-**ah**-nah
waitress	**cambrera**	kam-**breh**-ruh
waiter	**cambrer**	kam-**breh**
menu	**la carta**	lah **kahr**-tuh
fixed-price menu	**menú del dia**	muh-**noo** thuhl **dee**-uh
wine list	**la carta de vins**	lah **kahr**-tuh thuh **veens**
glass of water	**un got d'aigua**	oon **got dah**-ee-gwah
glass of wine	**una copa de vi**	**oo**-nuh **ko**-pah thuh **vee**
bottle	**una ampolla**	**oo**-nuh am-**pol**-yuh
knife	**un ganivet**	oon gun-ee-**veht**
fork	**una forquilla**	**oo**-nuh foor-**keel**-yuh
spoon	**una cullera**	**oo**-nuh kool-**yeh**-ruh
breakfast	**l'esmorzar**	les-moor-**sah**
lunch	**el dinar**	uhl dee-**nah**
dinner	**el sopar**	uhl soo-**pah**
main course	**el primer plat**	uhl pree-**meh** plat
starters	**els entrants**	uhlz ehn-**tranz**
dish of the day	**el plat del dia**	uhl **plat** duhl **dee**-uh
coffee	**el cafè**	uhl kah-**feh**
rare	**poc fet**	**pok fet**
medium	**al punt**	ahl **poon**
well done	**molt fet**	mol **fet**

Menu Decoder

l'aigua mineral	lah-ee-gwuh mee-nuh-**rahl**	mineral water
sense gas/ amb gas	sen-zuh gas/ am gas	still sparkling
al forn	ahl **forn**	baked
l'all	**lahl**yuh	garlic
l'arròs	lahr-**roz**	rice
les botifarres	lahs **boo**-tee-fah-rahs	sausages
la carn	lah **karn**	meat
la ceba	lah **seh**-buh	onion
la cervesa	lah-sehr-**ve**-sah	beer
l'embotit	lum-boo-**teet**	cold meat
el filet	uhl fee-**let**	sirloin
el formatge	uhl for-**mah**-djuh	cheese
fregit	freh-**zheet**	fried
la fruita	lah froo-**ee**-tah	fruit
els fruits secs	uhlz froo-**eets** seks	nuts
les gambes	lahs **gam**-bus	prawns
el gelat	uhl djuh-**lat**	ice cream
la llagosta	lah lyah-**gos**-tah	lobster
la llet	lah **lyet**	milk
la llimona	lah lyee-**moh**-nah	lemon
la llimonada	lah lyee-moh-**nah**-thuh	lemonade
la mantega	lah mahn-**teh**-gah	butter
el marisc	uhl muh-**reesk**	seafood
la menestra	lah muh-**nehs**-truh	vegetable stew
l'oli	**loll**-ee	oil
les olives	luhs oo-**lee**-vuhs	olives
l'ou	**loh**-oo	egg
el pa	uhl **pah**	bread
el pastís	uhl pahs-**tees**	pie/cake
les patates	lahs pah-**tah**-tuhs	potatoes
el pebre	uhl **peh**-bruh	pepper
el peix	uhl **pehsh**	fish
el pernil	uhl puhr-**neel**	cured ham
salat serrà	suh-**lat** sehr-**rah**	
el plàtan	uhl **plah**-tun	banana
el pollastre	uhl poo-**lyah**-struh	chicken
la poma	la **poh**-mah	apple
el porc	uhl **pohr**	pork
les postres	lahs **pohs**-truhs	dessert
rostit	rohs-**teet**	roast
la sal	lah **sahl**	salt
la salsa	lah **sahl**-suh	sauce
les salsitxes	lahs sahl-**see**-chuhs	sausages
sec	sehk	dry
la sopa	lah **soh**-puh	soup
el sucre	uhl-**soo**-kruh	sugar
la taronja	lah tuh-**rohn**-djuh	orange
el te	uhl teh	tea
les torrades	lahs too-**rah**-thuhs	toast
la vedella	lah veh-**theh**-lyuh	beef
el vi blanc	uhl **bee** blang	white wine
el vi negre	uhl **bee** neh-gruh	red wine
el vi rosat	uhl **bee** roo-zaht	rosé wine
el vinagre	uhl bee-**nah**-gruh	vinegar
el xai/el be	uhl **shah**ee/uhl beh	lamb
la xocolata	lah shoo-koo-**lah**-tuh	chocolate
el xoriç	uhl shoo-**rees**	red sausage

Numbers

0	zero	**seh**-roo
1	un (masc)	oon
	una (fem)	**oon**-uh
2	dos (masc)	dohs
	dues (fem)	**doo**-uhs
3	tres	trehs
4	quatre	**kwa**-truh
5	cinc	seeng
6	sis	sees
7	set	set
8	vuit	**voo**-eet
9	nou	**noh**-oo
10	deu	**deh**-oo
11	onze	**on**-zuh
12	dotze	**doh**-dzuh
13	tretze	**treh**-dzuh
14	catorze	kah-**tohr**-dzuh
15	quinze	**keen**-zuh
16	setze	**set**-zuh
17	disset	dee-**set**
18	divuit	dee-voo-**eet**
19	dinou	dee-**noh**-oo
20	vint	**been**
21	vint-i-un	been-tee-**oon**
22	vint-i-dos	been-tee-**dohs**
30	trenta	**tren**-tah
31	trenta-un	**tren**-tuh oon
40	quaranta	kwuh-**ran**-tuh
50	cinquanta	seen-**kwahn**-tah
60	seixanta	seh-ee-**shan**-tah
70	setanta	seh-**tan**-tah
80	vuitanta	voo-ee-**tan**-tah
90	noranta	noh-**ran**-tah
100	cent	sen
101	cent un	sent oon
102	cent dos	sen dohs
200	dos-cents (masc)	dohs-**sens**
	dues-centes (fem)	**doo**-uhs sen-tuhs
300	tres-cents	trehs-**senz**
400	quatre-cents	kwah-truh-**senz**
500	cinc-cents	seeng-**senz**
600	sis-cents	sees-**senz**
700	set-cents	set-**senz**
800	vuit-cents	voo-eet-**senz**
900	nou-cents	noh-oo-**cenz**
1,000	mil	meel
1,001	mil un	meel oon

Time

one minute	un minut	oon mee-**noot**
one hour	una hora	oo-nuh **oh**-ruh
half an hour	mitja hora	**mee**-juh **oh**-ruh
Monday	dilluns	dee-**lyoonz**
Tuesday	dimarts	dee-**marts**
Wednesday	dimecres	dee-**meh**-kruhs
Thursday	dijous	dee-**zhoh**-oos
Friday	divendres	dee-**ven**-druhs
Saturday	dissabte	dee-**sab**-tuh
Sunday	diumenge	dee-oo-**men**-juh